Hailey's Story

Hailey's Story

Hailey Giblin

with

Stephen Richards

JOHN BLAKE

Published by John Blake Publishing Ltd,
3, Bramber Court, 2 Bramber Road,
London W14 9PB, England

www.blake.co.uk

First published in hardback in 2006

ISBN 1 84454 191 6

British Library Cataloguing-in-Publication Data:

A catalogue record for this book is available from the British Library.

Design by www.envydesign.co.uk

Printed in Great Britain by Creative Print and Design

3 5 7 9 10 8 6 4 2

Papers used by John Blake Publishing are natural, recyclable products
made from wood grown in sustainable forests. The manufacturing
processes conform to the environmental regulations of the country
of origin.

Every attempt has been made to contact the relevant copyright-holders,
but some were unobtainable. We would be grateful if the appropriate
people could contact us.

For Colin, my saviour.

ACKNOWLEDGEMENTS

FIRSTLY, I WOULD LIKE TO THANK MY 'FUNNY GRANDDAD' – THANK YOU FOR BEING MY BEST FRIEND THAT NO ONE CAN REPLACE. You *really* are the brightest star in the sky. God Bless and Rest in Peace.

A special thanks to my newfound friend Lisa, who has helped me find 'Hailey' again. For that I am truly grateful.

I also want to thank my good friends Shaun and Angela, who have never judged. Thanks.

Thanks to Patrick Anderson, not only a good friend but also a great photographer, who has given me countless pieces of advice and still does so.

Thank you to the Reverend Brian East, who made my wedding day a day I will never forget.

A very special thanks to ChildLine for giving me the support I needed as a child.

A big thanks to a very special gentleman whom I greatly admire, Stephen Richards, the man with the golden pen.

And finally, my saviour, the man with a golden heart – Colin. Without you, I wouldn't be where I am today. A million thank yous.

CONTENTS

INTRODUCTION

BEHIND THE SEEMINGLY INNOCENT MASK OF A SCHOOL CARETAKER SIMMERED THE TICKING TIME BOMB OF A SERIAL RAPIST OF VULNERABLE YOUNG GIRLS, A MAN UNKNOWN TO THE WORLD AT LARGE UNTIL HE FOUND INFAMY AS THE SOHAM MURDERER.

Despite past accusations of rape against him, a catalogue of controversial police blunders masked allegations that Ian Huntley had paedophilic tendencies. And, when, on 4 August 2002, he could no longer suppress the malevolence festering within him, he killed Jessica Chapman and Holly Wells, both aged ten.

Allegations of Huntley's sexual obsession with young girls can be traced back to August 1995, when the family of a schoolgirl claimed that he had had sex with her. And yet, even though both the police and social services were to receive a string of accusations of rape against him over the years, he was still able to find work at a school, close to the very innocence of childhood.

News of the guilty verdict against Huntley for the Soham murders was not surprising when it was delivered in December 2003. Even so, the allegations against him that had surfaced in court caused shock waves of repulsion to sweep across Britain. People were appalled to find out that between 1995 and 1999 there were four accusations against Huntley of underage sex with girls of between 13 and 15, three rape allegations and one of indecent assault against an 11-year-old girl, Hailey Edwards.

The nation's fury was aroused when it was learned that Huntley may have abused the innocence of each of these girls. However, a lack of evidence and the refusal of some of the alleged victims to press charges against him had made it impossible for investigators to establish guilt.

Between August 1995 and July 1998, Huntley was reported to what is now North East Lincolnshire Social Services on five occasions: once for the alleged indecent assault and four times for allegedly having sex with underage girls, one 13 years old, the others 15. But each time social workers began investigating, Huntley, with incredible ease, would move on and pick up another girl. His charmed evasion of charges was possible because, amazingly, no link was made between the cases. Each was dealt with by different social workers and social services kept no record of alleged offenders.

Nevertheless, three of the alleged cases of underage sex were passed on, independently of one another, to the Humberside Police when, in August 1995, an allegation against Huntley of sex with a schoolgirl was made by her family.

Then, in April 1996, after a family reported their concerns to her school, social services became aware of another girl, Emma Fish, who was involved with Huntley. However, the girl refused to speak to social workers and avoided them, and after she was seen by her GP it was decided there was no need for social workers to be further involved.

Huntley's next conquest was 14-year-old Janine Oliver. It has subsequently been claimed that she lost her virginity to Huntley sometime in 1995, but it was not until the following year that she started going out with him, after he won her over with cheap cider and initiated sex. In May 1996, not far off the age of consent and determined to leave home, she refused to file a complaint – even though Huntley was cheating on her with her friends – and the police dropped their investigation.

That same month, the mother of a young girl, Louise Tinmurth, went on the warpath when her 12-year-old daughter met Huntley at a funfair. She claimed that Huntley once locked her in a room and demanded sex but she escaped. When social services interviewed her, she denied any sexual impropriety and said that she and Huntley were simply friends.

Then there was a 15-year-old who claimed that Huntley had kept her under lock and key during their six-month relationship and starved her for two weeks, after which she collapsed and was eventually taken to hospital. She also gave an account of Huntley sleeping with over 200 girls and said that it was control he sought rather than sex. None of these allegations led to Huntley being charged with any criminal offence.

In May 1996, two further allegations against Huntley were reported to social services by the families of other girls.

The following year, Huntley began a relationship with a 15-year-old, Katie Webber. Soon she became infatuated and said later, 'Once it was clear I liked him and we'd had sex, he began to treat me like a child, to bully me.'

In July 1998, 12-year-old Hailey Edwards reported to the Humberside Police an indecent assault that she alleged Huntley had committed against her in September of the previous year, when she was 11. After investigating the claim, the police decided not to send a file to the Crown Prosecution Service (CPS).

This allegation was made just a few weeks after Huntley had appeared in court in Grimsby, charged with raping another girl, a petite 18-year-old. On 22 May 1998, he was remanded in custody to the Wolds Prison at Everthorpe, Lincolnshire, before being granted bail on 30 May, when he secured a place in a bail hostel in Scunthorpe.

Then, on 30 June, after Huntley had stood in the dock at Grimsby Magistrates' Court for a second time, new evidence came to light. In view of this, the CPS decided it no longer had a strong enough case against him in respect of the charge of rape and the case was discontinued.

Only a few months before, on 7 January 1998, Huntley had appeared at Grimsby Crown Court, charged with a quite different offence: burgling a neighbour's house in Florence Street, Grimsby, in November 1995, with an accomplice called Jimmy Dean. The charge was that Huntley and Dean had stolen perfume, jewellery, a Black & Decker heat gun and £20 after breaking into the property, which adjoined Huntley's home, through a shared roof space.

The decision by the prosecution and the judge to allow the matter to 'lie on file' meant that, when police checks were made on Huntley after he applied for the caretaker's job at Soham Village College, he was found to have no criminal convictions. A senior officer involved in the Soham murder investigation described the decision as 'bizarre'.

What beggars belief is that, even though it is alleged that, between 1995 and 2001, he had a relationship or sexual involvement with seven girls in northeast Lincolnshire, all of them under the age of 16 and all known to one or more of the statutory agencies, there was never sufficient evidence to establish any criminal offence.

Another woman is said to have reported Huntley to the police for having had sex with her underage daughter. The complaint was made when the girl was 17, but the police have no record of it.

Huntley was also suspected of four alleged rapes, in April and May 1998 and May and July 1999. In connection with the last of these, his former partner, Maxine Carr, gave an alibi for Huntley, just as she did some three years later, when her false testimony was to earn her time behind bars.

To return to 1995, as early as August of that year Huntley had a 13-year-old boy and the boy's 15-year-old sister living with him at 16a Florence Street, Grimsby. After the children's father caused a disturbance at the door and allegedly 'cuffed' his son, the police were called. It is claimed that the man told police that Huntley had had unlawful sexual intercourse with his daughter, which the girl admitted. The following day PC Teasdale interviewed Huntley under caution at his home. During the interview, Huntley admitted having had the relationship with the girl and knowing that she was under 16, but said that 'if her parents were OK about it, it was not an offence'.

Huntley escaped charges, the police say, because the girl refused to lodge a complaint. This stands in stark contrast to how Hailey Edwards's boyfriend and eventual husband

Colin Giblin was later pursued and charged with unlawful sexual intercourse despite the fact that Hailey also did not make a complaint – it was her parents.

In February 1996, Huntley had a 15-year-old girl living with him in the flat he was sharing with his mother above a shop at 375 Pelham Road, Immingham, near Grimsby. Some two weeks later, the girl was reported to the Educational Welfare Officer by Kevin Huntley, Ian Huntley's father, as having come to stay with him and Ian three days before at another address in Pelham Road.

The referral to social services was passed on to an unqualified social work assistant in Grimsby West's Assessment and Investigation Team, Vicki Robertson, on 5 March 1996. There is no record of any checks having been made on either Ian or Kevin Huntley, and no record of any action taken. On 21 May, Sue Kotenko, of Grimsby East's Assessment and Investigation Team, gave the go-ahead to close the case. Again Ian Huntley was free to carry on as before.

In April of that year, Huntley was living with another 15-year-old girl at 16 Pelham Road, the address his father had given to an Educational Welfare Officer. Social services simply advised the girl's mother to exercise her parental responsibilities and 'get the girl home'. Soon afterwards, it is claimed, the mother went to Ian Huntley's home and threatened him with a knife, told him to leave her daughter alone and took her home. This sequence of events is revealed by a statement made by the girl.

At this time, both the girl and Huntley admitted to her mother that they were sleeping together. By now alarm bells should have been ringing very loudly and radical intervention by the police should have occurred.

In May 1996, there were two referrals to social services in respect of allegations that a 13-year-old girl had allegedly been coerced into having sex with Huntley, and there are police records of the interviews. The girl denied having had sex with Huntley, with the result that he was not questioned about the matter by the police. Later, both the girl and her mother stated that contact had occurred between Huntley and the girl when she was, in fact, 11, in 1993 or 1994, while Huntley was still with his wife. Subsequently, the girl claimed she had unlawful sexual intercourse with Huntley when she was 13.

In April 1997, there is evidence which suggests that Huntley had another 15-year-old girl living with him, but an allegation by her mother of unlawful sexual intercourse was not followed up and again Huntley was free to continue as before.

In September of that year, a 15-year-old schoolgirl claimed she had sexual intercourse with Huntley while in someone else's house. Her school seemed to be interested only in the fact that she had truanted, however. In October, the girl reported to social services that she had had sex with Huntley but that afterwards she had been warned off by two other girls.

The same social worker was involved as had been back in April. Yet, incredibly, no one in social services spotted the same name, Huntley, and again there are no records to show that either the social worker or the girl's school passed the details on to the police. Another missed opportunity.

It was six years later, in December 2003, that 29-year-old Huntley was convicted of murdering Jessica Chapman and Holly Wells. On that day, the then Home Secretary, David Blunkett, announced that an inquiry, headed by Sir Michael Bichard, would look into why the earlier accusations against Huntley were not brought to the forefront, and into the vetting system that had failed to prevent Huntley from getting a job as a school caretaker.

The Bichard Inquiry opened on 13 January 2004. After investigations lasting some five weeks, it found that critical errors had been made by the Humberside and Cambridgeshire Police Forces and by other organisations involved in the intelligence network. Miscommunication between the agencies handling the cases, as well as procedural flaws, were blamed for the fact that most of the complaints against Huntley were never linked together. There were even claims by the BBC that some of the reports of sexual assaults that were sent to Humberside's divisional intelligence bureau were accidentally deleted during a routine 'weeding' of the records by civilian staff in July 2000.

Had the reports been able to link all the allegations together, investigators would probably have been alerted to the cloud of suspicion that hung around Huntley and may have prevented the deaths of Holly and Jessica.

Another crucial problem was errors made by the Cambridgeshire Police in their use of their 'check system', which allowed Huntley to get a job at Soham Village College. It was widely reported that, during police background checks into Huntley on a national police database, his name and date of birth were entered incorrectly, so that no criminal history was revealed. Huntley's employers would later claim that, had they known about his past, he would never have been hired by the school.

As a result of Bichard, new, more rigorous vetting procedures were supposedly introduced. However, a disturbing case that has been tried since Huntley's conviction calls into question the effectiveness of these new measures. In the mid-1980s, Raymond Newell was given a job as a school caretaker by Gwent County Council at Bryn Primary School in Pontllanfraith, South Wales, despite his criminal record. Unsuspecting parents and teachers had, at that time, no idea that Newell, then in his late fifties, had a record of violence and dishonesty stretching back 46 years. This included three violent assaults, one on a police officer for which he was jailed for nine months in 1969. In 1981, just a few years before he became a school caretaker, he had been fined for causing actual bodily harm.

Just as Huntley did, Newell lured children into the school where he worked when it was empty at weekends. In October 2005, Cardiff Crown Court found Newell guilty of seven of the ten sexual assaults he was charged with. The victim, a pre-teenage girl who was not a pupil at Bryn Primary School, had described how the caretaker pulled down her clothing and his own before rubbing himself against her.

Just as Huntley tried to lie his way out of responsibility for the Soham murders, Newell, who had use of a caretaker's bungalow in the grounds of the school as a perk of his job, claimed the girl was making it all up. To expose the hollowness of Newell's denial, his distressed victim had to use a video link to the courtroom to give evidence to the court and be cross-examined.

Cardiff Crown Court heard that over an 18-month period Newell sexually assaulted a girl who was 12 when the assaults began. He abused her at weekends in his bungalow at the school and in the school's main building.

Just as Huntley admitted, in a police interview, his sexual misconduct with a minor, so did Newell. The court also heard how the twice-divorced caretaker lured children other than the girl into the school at weekends when it was empty.

Sentencing Newell to a paltry three years behind bars,

Judge William Gaskell said, 'You are going to prison. You will now have to expect that you will not be around for a long time.' Incomprehensibly, the judge even bailed Newell over the weekend in what he termed 'an act of mercy' that would enable the convicted man to speak to his elderly mother before being locked up. What act of mercy did the evil Newell show his young victim?

The same errors that allowed Huntley to kill also allowed Newell to destroy a little girl's life. No lessons at all had been learned from the Soham murders.

Hailey's cries of pain and anguish when she claimed in the summer of 1998 that he had 'raped' her some months earlier were felt to be insufficient by the police to prosecute on. If only Huntley had been stopped then.

Although the 12-year-old's innocent definition of rape was different from an adult's, Hailey had indeed been sexually assaulted in a nightmarish and drawn-out ordeal. Over several hours, Huntley repeatedly sexually abused Hailey after luring her away from the safety of her street in broad daylight and taking her to a secluded orchard behind a pub.

Although the jailing of Huntley for murder would eventually come, for Hailey, one of his youngest victims, there was no court case and so no justice to bring to an end the pain and humiliation she had suffered at his hands.

On 16 July 1998, Sue Kotenko, of Grimsby East's Assessment and Investigation Team, received from the police Form 547, which alleged Hailey had been assaulted by a 22-year-old man called 'Ian'. On 5 August, however, Police Sergeant Tait decided not to prosecute Huntley, on the grounds that there was insufficient evidence for there to be a realistic prospect of conviction. Huntley's bail was cancelled.

Seven months after Huntley's conviction for the Soham murders, Sir Christopher Kelly's North East Lincolnshire Area Child Protection Committee Report on the Huntley case, which covered the period 1995 to 2001, robustly criticised both the relevant police and social services for their incompetence. The Kelly Report of July 2004 revealed that a management review by social services acknowledged major concerns over the handling of the case. Further blame was laid firmly at the door of social workers for their failure to seek any additional information about Hailey at the time she reported Huntley's alleged assault on her.

Also commented on by the report were the circumstances of the alleged sexual assault, including Hailey's age, the location of the attack, its violent nature and the time lapse between its occurrence and its being reported. Together, Kelly stated, these should have generated questions in the minds of social services staff about the young girl's welfare.

The report went on to say, 'There appears to have been no attempt to consider MN [Hailey] as a potential or actual child in need in terms of Section 17 of the Children Act but rather to view the matter as an issue of crime detection.' And it further shamed social services and police by stating, 'Apart from anything else, alarm bells should have been rung by the circumstances in which the allegation came to light.'

Important as Kelly's findings were, they provided little consolation for Hailey, whose peace of mind had been shattered by the destruction of her innocence. Despite this, and the consequent harm she inflicted on herself, she earnestly tried to rebuild her faith in life by eventually marrying the man who had become her saviour when she ran away with him at the age of 15.

In a blaze of publicity, Hailey Edwards wed Colin Giblin, then 37, in Humberston, Lincolnshire, less than 18 months after Colin faced charges of unlawful sexual intercourse with the underage Hailey. What might have been merely an escape route from the pain of a stolen childhood seemed to Hailey a divine intervention, rescuing her from the hell she had endured.

Here was sanctuary and security in the arms of a man she trusted and loved. Yet the hell was to continue a little longer after Colin, having admitted unlawful sexual intercourse with Hailey, was, bizarrely, placed on the Sex Offenders' Register. After two weeks, when police accepted that he shouldn't have been on the register, his name was removed.

Here was the very essence of what love was all about being sullied, when the real cause of Hailey's living hell had been the subject of a whole raft of allegations of sex crimes that had been made known to the police and social services before the tragedy of Soham.

What of Huntley during the years that Hailey was hoping for justice? From July 1999, he seems to have gone to ground until he resurfaced in the Cambridgeshire village in 2002, with Maxine Carr (originally Capp).

It was on Sunday, 4 August that year that best friends Jessica Chapman and Holly Wells walked to a sports centre near their homes to buy sweets. The two ten-year-olds would not be seen alive again.

When the trial of Ian Huntley and Maxine Carr began at the Old Bailey in London on 3 November 2003, Huntley was seen as the primary culprit in the murders. After telling the court how he 'accidentally' killed the two girls, the accused said he tried to conceal the truth from his family, Carr and the police because of his shame and fear of not being believed.

Both Huntley and Carr were considered convincing liars and it was claimed in court that the girls 'had to die' in order to serve Huntley's own self-interest.

On 17 December 2003, the jury returned their verdict. Carr was found guilty of conspiring to pervert the course of justice, yet she was cleared of two counts of assisting an offender. She received a prison sentence of three and a half years.

After rejecting Huntley's story, the jury found him guilty of the murder of Jessica Chapman and Holly Wells. He was sentenced to two life terms in prison.

Another 18 months of waiting passed for Hailey Edwards and then, on 8 July 2005, following a further review of Huntley's alleged sex attack against Hailey eight years earlier, Catherine Ainsworth, a lawyer with the CPS in the Grimsby office wrote to advise her that they were not pursuing him over the matter. The three-page unsigned letter brought no comfort to Hailey as she read the lawyer's stark words: 'I have reviewed all of the evidence against Ian Huntley and have decided that there is not enough evidence to proceed with this case...'

Clearly, in reaching this decision, the CPS did not look at past allegations against Huntley or at the persuasive way in which he had lured Holly and Jessica to their deaths – much as he had sweet-talked Hailey into going to 'climb trees' when he had something much darker in mind.

And then, on 29 September 2005, the High Court set a 40-year tariff for Huntley, which means he must serve at least that length of time behind bars before even being considered eligible to apply for parole, by which time he will be almost 70.

Understandably, Hailey feels let down by Catherine Ainsworth's decision on behalf of the CPS. Consequently, she plans a civil prosecution against Huntley to prevent any attempt by him to gain freedom through gaining parole after serving his 40-year tariff. Here, in her own words, is Hailey's story.

1

WHEN THE SUN SHINES, EVERYONE IS HAPPY

ON 16 APRIL 1986, I WAS BORN IN THE FISHING PORT OF GRIMSBY. When I was delivered, in the Princess Diana Hospital, I weighed seven pounds and ten ounces, a little bundle of joy. I am the only girl of six children born to my mother. I have two younger brothers and three elder, all born in Grimsby.

By today's standards, if you go by the early-morning TV misery shows, my broken-home family of mixed-parentage siblings was quite normal. When my mum, Amanda Jayne Brown, was 16 she married David Lewis, and went on to give birth to her first child, Ben, and then, two years later, to Adam. After a marriage that lasted five years, she and David split up when they realised they were too young to hold on to the commitment. Anyway, that is what I was told. The boys kept the name Lewis.

Before long, my mother met David Baxter and soon after marrying him she gave birth to my brother Hayden. I was born next. The four-year marriage was destined for disaster. By this time I was nearly two years old. Even at this early age I was already broken-home material, fit for the likes of Jerry Springer's or Trisha's show.

Mum's split from David Baxter was an acrimonious affair that resulted in the family home being taken from us because of financial problems. After this, David Baxter went abroad with a woman.

If that wasn't bad enough, the aftermath of this break-up would follow me around for a few years, as you will see later. During Mum's estrangement from my father, she developed a relationship with a man called Wayne Edwards, and eventually I would accept him as my dad.

My mum's relationship with Wayne, a butcher in Humberston, started when she went into his shop and they got talking, and then, I suppose, it went from there.

At first, Wayne would visit my mum from time to time... he wooed her. He stayed over a few nights and then he would go back to his flat above the shop. After a while, my mum left the house in Northcoates, near Humberston, and moved in with Wayne, bringing me and my three brothers with her.

Once we were all in his flat, Wayne happily looked after his business and we accepted him as our stepfather. After four years, the relationship between him and Mum produced their first child, Joshua, and later their second son, Hadleigh, was born. These two were given the surname Edwards, as I was, because my mother used the name Edwards, although my birth certificate records my surname as Baxter. I remember I was lying down in the front room with my brother Hayden when Mum asked me, 'Would you like your name changed so that you have got the babies' last name as well?'

Mum asked my two eldest brothers, Ben and Adam Lewis, the same question, but they didn't want to because they were still in contact with their biological father on a friendly basis. He seemed to be a nice dad. All I know about her relationship with her first husband, David Lewis, obviously came from details she told me.

To this very day, Mum has stayed with Wayne. So I think the relationship she has got now with my stepdad is a strong one, a stronger one than those others. It has survived the test of time.

I would say that Mum is the one who wears the trousers in our household. That may well be what has made the relationship last. Wayne, not being a domineering man, is someone my mother can live with, which I mean in a good way. He has lost his temper with me on a few occasions – that's between him and me – but he has been good for my mum.

My first school was Cloverfields Primary and then I moved up to Humberston Comprehensive, which I thought was a lovely school until what happened to me when I was 11.

Just about everyone remembers their first day at school, as either one of happiness or one of sadness or fear. Mine, I'll never forget. I was moving up from day nursery to school. You were allowed to bring a teddy bear, because we had a teddy bears' picnic, and this girl had a toy thing in the shape of a ruler. One whack on your wrist and this thing would wrap itself around it.

We were playing Ring-a-Ring of Roses and this girl – her name was Emma Holmes – kept cracking this toy on her arm and the teacher, Mrs Braithwaite, said, 'Take that off your arm.' Eventually, the teacher took it off Emma and put it on her teddy bear.

We were going round in a circle and I pulled this toy off the teddy bear and started whacking it against my arm. I was playing with it for about ten minutes, but I didn't really get told off for it. Then Emma started crying and pointing at me, 'She's got my whip thing, she's got my whip thing.'

After that, I remember, I got a good telling-off for taking this wraparound toy when the other girl had already been told she couldn't have it. Try explaining that to a five-year-old. So my first day at school is etched on my memory, and it wasn't a good one.

That morning I'd tried to claw and scream my way out

of going to school. They said I screamed and screamed and screamed and didn't want to go. But, thankfully, I wasn't an introverted child, and my mum said that, as soon as I got inside the school and saw all the kids with their teddy bears and all that stuff, I was fine.

But Mum told me later that she went home crying because I'd screamed that much and was holding on to her neck. After that, she got my stepdad to take me to school in case I started crying again. Before long, though, I was all right and I progressed well at school. I am a great reader and at school they did an achievement task at the end of the year where you were assessed to find the best reader and the best writer. I was nominated the best reader for two years running.

When I think back to when I was really young, I recollect the bad things in life. I don't know if that is how I mark time – by putting dates to these sporadic events – but that is how history is remembered too: for all the bad things, wars, invasions, plagues, death. I mean, most people will be familiar with the dates of wars, but not with dates when great discoveries were made. Some know 1066 as being the year of the Battle of Hastings, but who can recall when Louis Pasteur discovered penicillin? As much as the Charge of the Light Brigade, the Battle of Trafalgar and the Battle of Britain are sacred to some, my past is even more sacred to me. We all recall historical dates connected with some dire act of misery. I'm no different in my personal memories.

One particularly strong memory I have is of the time my brother Hayden was playing with the coal fire. I was very young. That was when we lived in Northcoates with our biological father. I remember him sitting in his chair in the corner and my mum in the kitchen doing the dinner.

Hayden had this roll of sticky tape that he was rolling out and putting on the fire unsupervised. Without warning, he draped a flaming trail of fire on my wrist. As quick as a flash, I darted through the house towards the kitchen. I was a screaming, flaming Chucky doll with this roll of burning sticky tape stuck to my arm.

I can remember the strange, new, intense sensation of being burned by the blazing plastic. When I got to the kitchen, my mum plucked me up from the floor, put me on the sink and doused cold water on the burning flesh of my wrist. Not a fond memory.

This was no accident; call it a stupid prank, but I don't know many people who have suffered from the same sort of joke. The effect it had on me remains with me to this day. My brother's act was deliberate and has scarred my mind to the point where, although I didn't fall into the fire itself, I am very concerned for children going near an open fire.

Putting that negative and painful memory to one side, I do actually have, from time to time, one or two good flashbacks to the past. It's not all gloom and doom. I remember waking up in the morning and finding a dog on the end of my bed and then going downstairs, where there were even more presents to greet my searching eyes.

I remember the first time I saw Father Christmas, as he walked into the room trailing a black bin liner behind him. But there was something distinctly odd about him: he was wearing the full Father Christmas outfit, but with pointy, high-heeled shoes. Ladies' shoes! Mind you, at that age I still believed he was really Father Christmas. In fact, I didn't pick up on the high heels at first. I think it was Hayden who said, 'Look at Father Christmas's shoes,' and then my mum pointed it out and shrieked with laughter as she said, 'Yes, he *has* got funny shoes on.' I remember that, and that Christmas was the time I got a play kitchen.

Would you believe, it was only about a year ago that I learned the true identity of Father Christmas – well, the identity of *this* particular Father Christmas. It was my maternal grandmother, Joan. I found out from my auntie, my mum's sister, when I tricked her into telling me.

Although I considered myself to be a clever girl in the academic sense, I wasn't clever enough to question Father Christmas's high-heeled shoes. I was still pretty naïve and innocent in the ways of the world.

I always wanted to learn things. I was even keen to learn how to make a pot of tea. My nature was a giving one; I always wanted to do things to help people. I remember asking my mum and stepfather – from now on I'll call him my dad – for years, 'Can I make you both a cup of tea?' Every time they sternly said no because 'the kettle is hot' and 'the water is hot'.

Not one to be daunted by the prospect of a scalding, I kept suggesting that I make them a cup of tea, so when I got a little bit older and more able – I think I was about ten – I was allowed to. I skipped into the kitchen, joyful at the prospect of making my very first pot of tea. After I became competent, I would take an early-morning cup up to my mum in bed, and a coffee for my dad.

Mum would get up, put on her dressing gown and come downstairs and tidy up, whereas Dad would end up falling back to sleep and leave his coffee there to go cold for an hour. I would go to my bedroom and he would call out, 'Hailey, do me a favour, duck.'

'Yes, what's the matter?' I would ask enthusiastically.

'Will you make me a fresh cup of coffee? I'm sorry, I forgot that one,' my dad would groan.

'Yes, all right then,' I would chirp.

But after a couple of weeks I got bored with making hot drinks and Dad wasting his. So in the end, when he kept saying, 'Will you make me a fresh cup of coffee?', I would put on the kettle and while it was boiling I would place the cold cup of coffee in the microwave for 30 seconds to heat up. With the kettle boiling, they couldn't hear the noise of the microwave. I only told him about a year ago that I used to do this. I was a fast learner.

Although I was always looking to please people and was doing well at school, I always fell short of pleasing my mum in the sense that I didn't make her totally happy. Her disappointed outlook on life I put down to the fact that she may not have been wholly happy with her own lot, as she was really stressed with work. Mum is a workaholic.

Her job was as a care assistant, working in an old people's home all hours of the day and night. On reflection, I suppose juggling your life between work and your husband and six children must have been a bit of a balancing act. As a grown-up, I can see that nothing makes my mum happy. I don't want to sound like I'm attacking Mum's integrity, as she did congratulate me on my academic achievements, and she did attend school from time to time to see my work. But my gaining these qualifications didn't really please her in the way I felt it should have done.

In a way, I felt Mum never really supported me enough with homework, with subjects like maths. I used to enjoy maths until I was ten or eleven years old, but after that people used to say, 'You don't like maths, do you?' I would steadfastly defend myself, 'Yes, I really like maths and my maths teacher and everything.' I used to go home with homework and Mum used to say, with defeatism in her voice, 'Go and ask your dad... I'm not great at this, but your dad is good at maths.'

So Dad would sit there and say, 'I'll do it for you,' and he would do the work for me. But I look back on this now as the easy way out. You are supposed to say, 'Sit down and I will read the question out and you try and work out the answer,' instead of having someone else just write it down for you.

Mum was very busy with her work and I was the only girl. I felt that my brothers got everything and that my being asked to make the tea for everyone was a poor consolation prize. But then, for a while, things changed and for a good few years Mum and I became best friends and developed a loving relationship; we were inseparable.

Dad and Hayden used to do the father-and-son bonding routine of going to the football on a Saturday. Mum would get a can of Coke and a bag of bonbons and the two of us would sit there and watch repeats of *EastEnders*, do each other's hair or go out shopping. That's the sort of thing mums and daughters are supposed to do together, isn't it?

As I became older and more self-reliant, I fitted in with Mum's routine. At that stage I didn't feel neglected.

In trying to recall a spontaneous memory from that time, I remember the times I would be out in the street near to home. It's in part simply a fond memory and in part a growing-up memory that shows how I was starting to think for myself. The ice-cream man used to always come about ten minutes before teatime. Often

Mum would comfort me by saying, 'You can have an ice-cream tomorrow night, OK?' and then, 'Go on, you can go and play outside for ten or fifteen minutes and I'll shout for you when your dinner is done.'

Of course, I would catch sight of the ice-cream van and without hesitation I would saunter up to the van. Feasting my eyes on what was on offer, I'd have the brazen brainwave of saying to Don, the man serving, 'Oh, yeah, my mum hasn't got any change today, but she said, if she gives you the money tomorrow, could I, you know, have a cornet?'

Don would give in and say, 'Go on then, I'll give you an ice-cream.'

As I recall this, I remember how much I wanted that ice-cream. I wanted an ice-cream that minute, there and then, not tomorrow. That was as far as I pushed the boundaries of innocence as a child. I knew no different, but it shows how childhood innocence was looked upon by the ice-cream man.

I pulled that ruse quite often, but then Mum and Dad cottoned on and they would come out to the van and say to Don, 'Did Hailey have an ice-cream last week that she forgot to pay for?'

Don would innocently reply, 'Well, actually, she had about four' as he looked at me with that 'You're not supposed to do that' expression on his face.

When I got a little bit older, I used to do the same thing but the very next day, when the ice-cream man came, my mum would give me the money and I'd say to Don, 'Oh, there's the money for your ice-cream.'

I would say to Mum and Dad, 'Oh well, I don't want one tonight because I used the money for today's,' and they would say, 'Well, go on and have one anyway.'

Something that happened not long ago made me recall this particular memory. We went for a day out to Hemswell Market, where I used to go shopping with my granddad on a Sunday. I walked past an ice-cream van and I saw this guy inside and, to my utter astonishment, it was Don. It was the same ice-cream man, in the same van, and it brought the memories flooding back like a burst dam. And didn't it seem as if time had stood still? I was just standing there thinking, God, how strange is that after all these years?

I went straight over and said hello to him. To my amazement, he remembered who I was. He was like, 'God, I haven't seen you in ages. You look so grown up now. You've cut all your hair off.' My hair used to be down past my waist. It was like I had accelerated all these years forward to where I was now. God, if only that had been possible! I just stood there and I had a lot of fiery flashbacks. All these disjointed memories came flooding back.

That brings me on to a memory tinged with both happiness and sadness that was brought on by the memory of going to the market with Granddad. When

I was still in primary school, on Fridays my mum used to go to this fish and chip restaurant with her dad, Granddad Don, and Grandma. The place had the peculiar name of the Pea Bung – that's what Granddad used to call it, anyway. 'We're off to the Pea Bung on Friday,' he would pipe up.

When my mum got back I would eagerly ask, 'Did you have a good day, Mum?'

With a twinkle in her eye, she would reply, 'Yes, guess where I've been.'

'Where?' I'd say.

'Go on, have a guess,' she would challenge me.

Feeling I'd been left out, I would ask dejectedly, 'You haven't been to the Pea Bung with Granddad, have you?' Because as a child it was my favourite place.

Mum would bring me down but then lift me up by answering, 'Yes, I have, but next week we'll go, and we'll go on a Saturday.'

'Can't I go on a Friday?' I would plead.

It was always, 'No, you can't, because you've got school, so we'll take you on the Saturday instead.'

Still, the chance to go to the Pea Bung, even on a Saturday, was a treat beyond comprehension. The expectation of what lay ahead on Saturday would fill me with delight. To some the place was just a normal, everyday chip shop with a restaurant. But to me the Pea Bung embodied all that was good in the world: there I could sit, look out of the window and see the world go by while enjoying the company and a special treat from Granddad.

He would proclaim with gusto, 'Well, I'm going to have fish,' and, as he looked expectantly at my mum, he would ask, 'What are you going to have, Mandy?'

Mum would pick herself a mouth-wateringly tasty piece of fish from what was on display in the hot, glazed servery and, in turn, ask, 'What do you want, Hailey?'

Shivering with excitement, I would gather my thoughts and say, 'Can I have a small sausage, please, with chips?'

Within minutes my order would arrive in the safe hands of a waitress: two massive sausages, some big, fat beefy chips, peas, gravy and a thirst-quenching glass of orange juice to wash it all down, all accompanied by doorstops of bread and butter. It was a magical experience that words can't fully capture. 'Wow' might be the best word to describe it. And yet, from the outside, the place was nothing special. It was on the corner of Freeman Street, in Grimsby: a brick building with two windows. We used to sit near the window at the far end. The place had a strange sort of sliding door; and it was narrow, so only one person at a time could squeeze in.

We would go in and Granddad would announce regally, 'A table for three, please.' They would show you to a little high-sided booth. The booth was like Santa's sleigh: it instilled a feeling of sanctuary, even of womb-like security. That cafe, with its 'olde worlde' charm, meant a lot to me. There I was protected from all the evil in the world. So it meant more to me than just being ushered to our booth and sitting there, Mum, Granddad and I. I don't recall Grandma ever coming with us on a Saturday.

Afterwards, we used to have a gentle stroll around the wondrous marketplace and, to keep me contented for the trip home, they would buy me a small bag of sweets.

That's my special memory of the Pea Bung, an enchanted place that remains in my thoughts; a place that offered warmth, security and comfort. If I could wish myself back to anywhere in the world, that would be it.

The reverence I felt for it was destroyed, though, if anybody else came along with us, including my brothers. They were infringing on my special place, and it would infuriate me. This was my special world, and I would think, Don't you know, you shouldn't really be here. This is my place with Granddad and Mum.

I knew I was Granddad's favourite; he always called me special. I like to think so, anyway, because there were so many of us children. He used to give everyone else a normal-sized birthday card or Christmas card but, when it came to my birthday or Christmas, I would get a really big one from him and he would always write inside: 'To my darling Hailey, hope you have a wonderful birthday, my special girl, love from your Funny Granddad.'

We called him 'Funny Granddad' because he was a witty and amusing man. Everything he used to come out with was funny; he was just that extraordinary type of person.

As much as I would describe the Pea Bung as my sanctuary, I would describe my grandfather as my rock. However, nothing is forever, and, at 14, my world was to collapse soon enough. I remember being near the front door, when we lived in Glebe Road, in Humberston, and my cousin Keeley burst in, her face ashen. 'Where's your mum, where's your mum?' she wailed. She was crying her eyes out and in that split second I knew what had happened.

Granddad's death was a shock to us all: he wasn't ill and it was so sudden. He had a lady friend who lived around the corner and they used to go out shopping or he would go and have a natter and a cup of tea with her. From what I was told, he went round there one day and he was sitting in the front room having his regular cup of tea when he said to her, 'I don't feel very well, can I go for a lie down?' So he went and lay on her bed and, when she went to see if he was all right, he had died. He was seventy years old. My rock had crumbled.

That morning, before Granddad died – I think it was a Friday – Mum had mentioned going out for fish and chips at the Pea Bung. Mum had bought another house, as our finances were better, and she was planning on going there that morning to do some work. So it was a big surprise that she was thinking about taking Granddad to the Pea Bung, and I was under the impression that I might be able to go there this time. Sadly, it wasn't to be.

Since then, my memories of the Pea Bung have been tinged with dark clouds of sorrow, but fond rainbow-coloured memories still shine through like shafts of sunlight on a stormy day.

Many years later, I plucked up the courage to make a pilgrimage to the Pea Bung. My visit conjured up a mixed bag of memories. In a way, I felt proud of the cosy little place. Still there were the protective booths, the seats, the funny little door. One other thing I recall is that they had this unusual wooden spoon bearing the words 'Don, the world's biggest stirrer'.

I used to quiz Granddad about this. 'What does that mean?'

Amused, he would throw his head back and say with a laugh, 'I'll tell you when you get a bit older.'

I couldn't wait for the secret of the spoon to be revealed to me. Mum used to say that it was because he used to stir up trouble with all the little old ladies behind the counter and pull their leg and tell them jokes and try to mess about by saying things like, 'Well, she said this about you,' and they would go, 'Did she, really?' and then he would say, 'No, not really.' So they got a big spoon and put it on the wall for him.

Then, when we went back not long ago, I was devastated to see that the place I once worshipped had been changed. Its whole sanctity had been disturbed. The essence of what the Pea Bung was all about seemed to have been lost. Gone were the special Santa's sleigh seats, all knocked out and replaced with new seating. I felt quite uncomfortable. It sounds silly, because it was only a fish and chip shop, but it wasn't special any more, like it used to be. The charm had gone.

But I still ordered two sausages, chips, peas and gravy, a glass of orange juice and some bread and butter. Mind you, there was a small consolation when I was approached by some of the staff – half of them I didn't even know – and they declared, gobsmacked, 'You're Don's granddaughter!

'How old are you now?' they asked.

Then someone said, 'I remember you when you were six years old, sitting there, when you knocked over your glass of orange and the look on your face was just like "Oops".'

'Oh, did I?' I said.

They all remember me, although I don't know them. You can guarantee that every time I set foot in there they will go, 'Your granddad was called Don, wasn't he?'

'Well, I've never seen you before but yes he was, yes,' I say.

On that first return visit, I had a feeling of loss when I looked around for Don's 'stirrer spoon' and it wasn't there. I asked where it was and if I could have it, and they told me, 'Come back when we have sorted the shop out and you can have that.'

The lady said it had been taken down only about three or four weeks earlier, because they were changing everything around. When I went back again, they had clearly made the changes to the place, but the spoon still wasn't there. And that was that.

That day Granddad died, Mum and I were alone in the house after Keeley had left. Mum sat on the stairs crying her eyes out, and I was crying beside her. I reached out and put my arms around her. I felt enormously upset, as if my world would explode in a million pieces. It was just Mum and I. So I thought, Well, I'm going to look after her because nobody else is here. That is the feeling I think I had from that time on.

Losing my granddad in my early teens had an overwhelming and disturbing effect on me. The loss of such a strong alpha male from my life left a void, a chasm so hollow that even the moon could not fill it. I ached and ached until there was nothing but hollow numbness within me.

Granddad made me feel safe; he was like a best friend. I couldn't do anything to disappoint him. Whenever I was around him I was always good and behaved myself, but out of respect, not fear. He insulated me from the pain I will tell you of later. Although I minded my Ps and Qs around Granddad, I never had to stand on ceremony.

I was talking to my friend not so long ago about it, and I realise the amount of respect that I showed Granddad was overwhelming: I would have licked the mud off his boots. And yet, for all the respect I showed him, I didn't show enough to others around me. Basically, all the respect went to this one man. In my eyes, he was the only one worth it. And I felt that he respected me just as much as I did him.

My idea of dying is illustrated by the way you see some elderly people who are content to be able to say that their family has grown up safe and well. I will be the silly old woman contentedly baking cakes, in maybe about 70 years' time.

Shattered as my world was, somehow I had to piece it all together again and get on with life. I found it really hard to deal with losing Granddad because he was the only one I wanted to be close to. Through his love and understanding of me at that time, he gave me something that nobody else was able to. I felt special around him. I felt that I was not just being loved; I felt a love between us that was paramount, one that lasted because I was his favourite one.

After Granddad died, I felt that I wasn't anyone's special one, and nobody came to my rescue. I used to think he would always be there for me and I would always be there for him. When it came to the finality of accepting he was dead, I still hadn't come to terms with the loss. And I think that contributed to my going off the rails. There was no one to give that same amount of respect to. I had no reason to be on my best behaviour any more.

In relation to what I went through at such a young age, the message I would send out to children of a similar age would be to try to take a leaf out of their loved one's book, like I did with my granddad. If I tried to be a person who was just as good as him and treated people with respect and they didn't give it to me in return, then fine. But at least I was showing it to them. I was trying to do the best that I could for other people, just as Granddad did. I try to treat them with respect, as he did towards me. Don't judge a book by its cover.

Thinking about how that wisdom could be applied today, when values have changed so much in such a short space of time, I realise relationships seem not to be valued as they once were. But the grandparent–grandchild relationship can be invaluable if one party can inspire respect in the other and vice versa. This relationship of mutual respect could play an important role for today's teenagers, faced by the pressures of modern life, especially the lure of drugs and violence.

My experience is that grandparents have an important role to play in the development of the core values that were once held by the majority of people, not the minority, as appears to be the case now. I remember one time I was sitting at my aunt's house and I kept kicking the settee and my mum told me off, saying, 'Don't do that, please.' Granddad came in and I was thinking, How far can I push it? He came over and put his hand firmly on my knee and said persuasively, 'Don't do that, please.' I thought, Oh, I've been told off by Granddad. I was able to learn right from wrong, and the respect I had for him played an important role in that learning process. Respect helps people learn right from wrong, whereas the imposition of a domineering person's will to force another to learn something is, I believe, how rebels against society are made.

The central point is that, out of love and respect for someone else, people can turn their own life around and even challenge society's bad guys. But I know that, as much as I had respect from my grandfather when he lived, in some sense it died with him. So I had to become strong within myself. My idea of becoming strong may have been slightly distorted because of the predominantly male influence in my life. I couldn't very well exchange my feminine skills for harder, masculine ones.

I do know that, when Granddad passed away, I felt deserted, as if he had been a traitor to me, had let me down and done me wrong by dying. I just thought that my world had come to an end. I was obviously angry that he had left me, and I thought, Well, you were supposed to be here for ever, to look after me and make sure that nothing bad happens to me again.

Whether or not it was because I was younger when Grandma died – I was just six then – I don't know, but Granddad's death had far more impact on me. I know that Catholics like to see the body before it is interred, and, although my faith is Church of England, I recall seeing Granddad lying in the Chapel of Rest before going to his funeral to pay my last respects. I had to come to terms with my anger at him for leaving me. When I set eyes on him laid to rest, my world fell apart again, but he had drilled into me that, when you die, you go up to heaven, and he used to always say that about Grandma.

Sometimes he used to talk about Grandma and he would announce, 'Oh, it's raining again,' and I would say, 'Yeah, I know,' and he would muse, 'Well, that's your grandma up in heaven, washing the floors and all the water is dripping down.' At other times he'd say, 'It's sunny today. Everyone is having a good time up there, they're having a party. When the sun shines, everyone is happy.'

I always remember he used to tell me, 'Oh, Grandma's not very happy today because the clouds have come out. She's not very happy, don't want to know us today.' I suppose it was a collection of nice memories. He didn't just say, when you die you're dead. He treated death with respect and humility.

So when I went to see him in the Chapel of Rest I was able to relate to what he had said about death. It was sunny the day we went to see him, so I thought, He must be up there and he must be happy, the sun is out, he must be having a party. A lot of my anger dissipated when I went to see him. I'm pleased I did.

With regard to going to see a loved one before he or she is buried or cremated, I think that is down to everyone's individual needs, but for me it was right, as young as I was. I was asked whether I would like to go or not, and I made the decision myself. Straight away I said yes. And I was proud that I saw Granddad in his best suit.

I remember he was obsessed with frogs. As you walked through the door of his porch, a frog noise greeted you, which always made me giggle. Every time I walked in I would say, 'That silly frog, he's everywhere.' Granddad even used to have black socks with frogs on, and things like that, right to the end. So he took his humour, this fun side of him, to the grave. Thanks for everything, Granddad.

2

JORDAN'S ATTITUDE TO LIFE AND CATHERINE ZETA-JONES'S WAY OF LIVING

WHEN I'D COME TO TERMS WITH THE LOSS OF MY GRANDDAD, MY SCHOOL LIFE WAS CERTAINLY OK. And I was starting to excel in sports: I was good at rounders and cross-country running… well, it wasn't like cross-country when I was in primary school, it was more like a fun run around the field. As I got older I grew to love netball, which was my main sport.

What really inspired me to play my best was the other girls' cattiness and negativity. They used to say I was no good at netball, but if I got angry or if someone said, 'You can't do this, you can't play,' then I would be able to play and that was enough to shut my critics up. I'll show you, I used to think. I'm just under five feet nine, and when I was younger I used my height to full

41

advantage. The teacher, Mrs Gooseman, used to say that I was a great netball player and I used to feel proud afterwards, thinking, Yes, I can play, never mind everybody saying I can't.

I'd started playing netball when I was about nine and I carried on until I was about fourteen. Around that time I stopped this and my other sports, too, though I still quite enjoy jogging and the odd hour in the gym. At that age I did all the usual girlie things with my friends. In particular I admired Geri Halliwell, though nobody else in my circle of friends really had Geri down as their favourite Spice Girl. They were all, 'Well, I like Posh Spice' and 'I like her, but we don't like that one,' meaning Geri.

To this sort of comment, I used to say, 'Well, I really like her, she is individual, she is her own sort of person. If she wants to dress in a Union Jack dress, then fine. She's cool; she's one of the Spice Girls.' And I would always confidently predict, 'When that band split up she will be the only one standing, because she has got something special about her.'

'No, no. She's rubbish,' they would say scornfully, and I used to think, with contempt, Well, people say that about netball and me, but at the end of the day, when you have scored three goals, that's what counts.

When the girls belittled Geri, I was able to equate my position to hers. I felt I was defending myself when I was defending Geri. I felt my alter ego was Geri

Halliwell and, by proxy, I was able to stand up for myself. In a way I felt obliged to defend Geri and I even sympathised with her – not that she would have batted an eyelid at the scorn these schoolgirls showed towards her. I often wondered what would happen if she were to pay a surprise visit to the school. I could just imagine the two-faced traitors licking up to her and gushing through false smiles and gritted teeth, 'Oh, Geri, we buy all your records. We love you, Geri.'

And I wouldn't let these same people get away with saying I was useless at netball. I did defend my ego, as that is what I am: a defender. I was able to stamp my authority on the game not just by winning but by scoring good points. By playing better and by proving to myself, rather than to others, that I was capable of achieving my own goals.

My ability to bounce back at this age was inspirational to me and spurred me on. I was young, vibrant and full of life. Just because someone would suggest that I wasn't good at something wouldn't put a damper on it. I wouldn't think, You've kicked me, I am down. I would think, I am getting back up, I am going to respond to that with my actions; I am going to show you that I am able to overcome adversity.

This wasn't just so that I could prove my resilience to others, not to prove them wrong or whatever, but to prove myself right, to prove that if I put my mind to something I could do it. It needn't have just been about netball, although that is what I have drawn on as an example.

I believe it was my family, in various ways, that helped me challenge those who said I was no good. They have never pushed me forward with calls of 'Come on, girl, we will support you in whatever you do.' I believe it is as a consequence of this lack of support that I have overcome certain put-downs. I am my own person. If I want something I won't rely on anybody to get it for me. I will go out there and work damn hard to get it myself so that people who may want to judge me can't say, 'She wouldn't have that if it wasn't for me.' I want to be able to stand on my own merits.

I wasn't born with a silver spoon in my mouth. Anything I get, earn or achieve is something that I have done myself. Whether that is as a direct result of mirroring my mum's efforts in working all hours and seeing what she can achieve, and she has bounced back from some tough situations, I don't know. But I do know that, when I reach 40, I don't want to be just a wife and a mum.

This determination isn't something that was instilled into me as a child. This is something that I just put into myself, thinking, I don't want to just be an ordinary mum. What could have influenced this belief was that my granddad always said that when I walked into a room everybody would look at me. 'Your eyes sparkle and everybody's face lights up,' he told me. 'You're special.'

I would like to think that I could influence people for the better. What my granddad told me, all the good things and all the praise, I feel that it did, in fact, work. Without that praise, without being patted on the back, 'Good girl, you have done well,' that effect on me may not have happened. I can say with certainty that my granddad's influence came through to me and made me a stronger person, but not straight away. It was something that permeated me slowly, that took time to mature to what it is today.

Self-praise is no praise. I can thank Granddad for showing me that. I remember how I would create something at school, maybe something I never really held aloft as a work of art, but Granddad would give a knowing look and cast his discerning eye over it and say, 'Oh, can I have that, please?'

That's how he was able to lay the foundations within me for the road ahead. I would say, 'Look at what I've done at school today, I have done this mosaic.' Of course, when Granddad asked for it, I used to think, Why, is it that good that he wants this on his fridge? It has got to be good, that's great. He would go on about the creative arts and making things.

Granddad had this pot – I think Mum has got it now – it was just a clay pot that I made. Everybody else was just making a normal bowl, but I made a square one, and it was really good. I would even be proud of it if I were to make it now. I cut out little leaves, made marks on them and put a row of them all the way around it. Then I painted it black, with the leaves in green. I was quite proud of that. Granddad ended up keeping it and I think when he died Mum put it in the cabinet.

Another time, when I was about 12, we were asked to look at something and be inspired by it. The art teacher just put a load of objects together – a clothes iron, some thick chain, a flower and other things – and said, 'I want you to draw what you see. Draw an impression of what you believe it represents.' He added, 'Don't just look at a picture, look deeper into the picture.'

My picture was massive, all bright colours, with the chain going right across the page. Mum's friend Dawn opened a café in Freeman Street and the owner's son did a similar painting and put it up in the café. Then she asked my mum if she could put my picture up, and she said no.

Mum had a nice frame and glass put on the picture. Then and there, the framer offered her £900 for it. Mum praised the work, cooing, 'That's what my daughter did in Year Eight.' When she came home she gushed, 'You know that painting, the man that I took it to said he would buy it for £900.' At the time I was cock-a-hoop and squealed with delight at the prospect of being rich. 'Oh, and are you going to sell it so that I can have some money?' I asked.

'No!' said Mum.

To this day the cherished painting hangs in Mum's house. I wasn't particularly inspired by any Impressionist painter, and to this day I have never painted another thing like it – it was a one-off. I didn't have an urge to go to art school or the like. I have got to be 110 per cent interested in something, because, if you are only 90 per cent interested, what's the point?

My hidden artistic talent was never applied to anything more than normal paintings that were just stuck on the fridge. But that Impressionist picture is quite inspired, and you wouldn't think I had created it. Whether it represented something in my life at that time, I don't know. Perhaps I was trying to reveal the brighter side of me, because I felt quite dull then. Maybe it represented something in my experience that I was only able to interpret artistically.

You could call it an Expressionist piece, because it was able to express what I couldn't put into words. In trying to find my thoughts from that period, I came up with: Everyone in this world has got friends and I am on my own, so I will paint this.

I used bright pink and yellow when everyone else was using black and dark green. As I look back, I think in that painting I brought out the way I was feeling then. My strong colours represented a lot of aspects missing in my life, and I was able to use art in a therapeutic way. It embodied everything that I felt I didn't have at that time: vigour, energy, power.

At that period in my life, everything seemed so uninspiring. This is why I looked at myself for inspiration; it sounds narcissistic, but I wasn't in love with myself. I felt that I was leading a humdrum, repetitive existence: school, home, homework, school. My escape from it all was to look at the Spice Girls as an example of what could be done to change your life. They were full of vigour and pep, particularly Geri Halliwell; she was the embodiment of all that I wanted to be. I felt I could have been her, so I defended her.

I liked Geri so much that, when we did a talent contest at Cloverfields Primary, I performed as her after getting together with some other Spice Girl wannabes. We had a month to rehearse as the group we wanted to be or to work at portraying a solo singing star. I enjoyed singing and I was doing Geri Halliwell's bit of 'Who Do You Think You Are'. So, in a way, I became my idol. I had my hair done and threw myself into the role when we performed on stage in front of the whole school.

A few years later, when I was about 13, I sang Mariah Carey's 'Hero', a solo song. I put a great deal of preparation into that role. I prepared myself about six months beforehand and got my outfit sorted, and on the day, as I went up on stage, I drew a hesitant breath. Everybody saw this performance: parents, children and teachers. In preparation for this role, my friend put my hair up in a spiral and I got dressed up to the nines. I'd never set my heart on becoming a singer: it just flowed out of me and I followed.

And then I wanted to be a singer. In fact, bizarre as it may sound, I wanted to be a singing model. 'How can you be a singing model?' people used to say. I would reveal my deepest desire, answering, 'Well, you stand there in front of the camera and have a few pictures done in the morning, nine till twelve, have some more pictures done and then, one till four, or something like that, you go and sing.'

From the age of seven I wanted to be a model. These svelte women parading the latest Paris fashions on the catwalk looked breathtaking. I guess that is every little girl's dream: to aspire to become something great, to achieve something special in life.

I didn't want to become subservient, I wanted to be an individual, because I saw all these women walking along the catwalk and I thought, I could do that, but I could do that better. I would really work hard to do that. So I wouldn't say anybody inspired me. Although if I had to pick someone with attitude, it would be someone like Jordan. In spite of the setbacks she has had in her life, she still comes back fighting and she doesn't hide from the public gaze. She is loud and outspoken, so, in a way, she could be a role model, but not because of her modelling; I didn't look at her because of that. I like her attitude to life: she won't be pushed about. Jordan sang in the Eurovision Song

Contest and, although she had a song knocked back, she was my ideal role model as a singer too.

I remember watching *America's Next Top Model* on TV, and the girl who won one of the shows was recruiting other girls: it was like a competition to become her protégée. But it wasn't just about looks, but the way she was as a whole. That girl's looks, Jordan's attitude and Catherine Zeta Jones's lifestyle add up to my ideal role model, the one I could truly aspire to be.

At the age of 11, I was caught between playing with my Barbie doll and experimenting with make-up, as most girls of that age do. I was the epitome of a beautiful little girl, with tresses of long, flowing hair, and I regularly wore party frocks on a Saturday.

From wanting to be a catwalk model, as I came into puberty I was changing my outlook on life. At times I would be happy being at home playing with my Barbie dolls and my teddy bears, and pushing my pram down the street.

That is how I was playing and doing my hair at 11. By 13, I was completely changed, with short hair, because of the things that had happened to me at the hands of Ian Huntley. But I don't want to go into that yet.

For two or three years, we lived in the cramped flat above the butcher's shop and then we moved to a three-bedroomed house, also in Humberston. I was living with my five brothers, my mother and my stepfather. One of the downstairs rooms had been converted into a fourth bedroom, and that was mine.

Life for me was one of protected innocence. On a Saturday Mum would say, 'Put your dress on, put your little shoes on.' With my flowing hair I was like a little Pear's Soap girl. People think they can't have a perfect child, but I was at that stage.

Around this time my dad went bankrupt and lost his butcher's business because, he said, Tesco had opened up just down the road and the new supermarket took his customers.

Mum was still a care worker, moving about within the industry. Dad was working for Kimberley Clark, the toilet-roll manufacturers, and also became a special constable. At home Mum was still the pack leader.

I don't recall having quality time as a family, trips out to the cinema or going out for a meal together. None of that close bonding family thing happened. I remember, though, when I was about 14, going to Ikea in Leeds with Mum, Dad and my two youngest brothers. And there was one family holiday, when I was about 12, when we went to Disneyland in Florida for two weeks. The two eldest boys stayed at home, so it was Mum, Dad, Hayden, Joshua, Hadleigh and me. It was fun, but I think they would all agree with me that Hayden monumentally ruined the holiday because he was just miserable throughout. He was just at that difficult age, two years older than me, and I don't think Disneyland was really for him.

The problem was that Hayden smoked and he was suffering withdrawal symptoms. He was dragging his heels and had to be practically hauled on to the plane. I must admit, he was excited to an extent, but then he wanted some cigarettes even though he couldn't smoke in front of my parents. I smoked as well. I don't think Mum knew this, but I believe she knew Hayden did.

Over 18 months, I had saved up money by taking two paper rounds, cleaning my next-door neighbour's car, tidying up and doing little jobs like that. I ended up with £500 for the holiday. Hayden had saved up roughly the same, but he had spent it all before we set off.

While we were in America, he kept demanding, 'Go on, ask that lady for a fag.'

I would snap, 'No, if you had saved your money, then you would have been able to go and buy some. No, I'm not going.'

Then he would sweet-talk me, 'Just go and ask her, please.'

'No, it's bloody cheeky.'

'No, no, no, it's not. Just go and ask her.'

'No. I'm not going to. If you wanted fags you should have saved up your money and bought some or brought some with you and stuck them in your bag.'

So Hayden was pretty miserable on that holiday, but

I enjoyed it and took in the whole Disney tour. It was a fond memory. It wasn't worthless or a wasted two weeks. It was better than a day trip to Ikea!

After that, the nearest I got to a close-knit family life was when I would sit in the front room with Mum and Dad and my two youngest brothers to eat my tea or dinner. But then the elder one would go to his bedroom to eat his and the younger one to his bedroom to do the same. It was a bit like the story of the three little piggies, each little pig with its own house to retreat to.

3

NOT SERIOUSLY WRONGED, THE CHILD TRUSTS THE FUTURE

DESPITE THIS LACK OF FAMILY COHESION, EVERYONE LIVED IN COMPARATIVE HARMONY WITH ONE ANOTHER. Although there were no big family fallouts or jealousy or fighting to be number one in the pack, Dad used to get annoyed with Ben, the eldest, because he used to be quite bossy towards me and my younger brothers. I think he thought he was an extra parent.

I remember when I was six years old, two of my brothers were in a bedroom and somehow a mirror got broken. Dad raced up to see what the noise was. Ben and Adam blamed me; they used me as a scapegoat. In anger, I charged through to my room – at this time my bedroom was upstairs – where I had a mattress on the floor, as we were waiting for beds to be delivered.

Dad stormed into my room after me with a look of thunder on his face. He took his slipper off and used it to smack me. It wasn't just like smack, smack and 'You're done, don't do it again.' I had never been assaulted before, but from the anger in his eyes I knew as he took his slipper off that something sinister was about to happen.

I was in fear, but what could I do at six years old against a grown man? I wanted to cry out that I wasn't responsible for the broken mirror but my voice was almost stifled by my fear. I just managed to cry out, 'It wasn't me. It wasn't me.'

There was no stopping my dad as, slipper in hand, he manhandled me and violently struck my bottom with the sole. In between each whack, and with perfect timing, he seethed through his clenched teeth, 'You will not sit down for a month, young lady.'

After he had finished dishing out the punishment, I was left there sobbing. My mother was out at work. I feel that if she had been at home at that particular time she would have taken an eye for an eye as far as my dad's actions were concerned. It wasn't until the following day that I was able to reveal the damage he had caused to me by showing her the purple, telltale welts that were the legacy of his fury.

With a rumbling rage that was barely hidden beneath her apparent calmness, Mum ordered me, 'Go upstairs.' The next thing I knew, World War III had broken out.

What did Dad expect? I seem to recall there was an apology from him when I came downstairs later on, but I am not totally sure about this, as it is the attack that remains in my mind more than what followed. I do remember my dad looking sheepish after having had the wrath of Mum inflicted upon him.

When she came home, she had picked up on the fact that something had gone on, because there was an atmosphere in the house. I was still upstairs in my bedroom, and the boys were still in theirs. To Mum, I was conspicuous by my absence, so she came upstairs and got out of me what had happened, and that is when it exploded into all hell.

After the carry-on with the slipper, I soon managed to bounce back the Hailey way and set about living the life of a normal little girl. I had experienced the humiliating pain of a punishment slippering for the first time.

But, with anything to do with sex, I was as innocent as a newborn baby. So, when a boy I knew tried to get me to perform a sexual act on him when I was eight years old, it was alien to me. The sex act he tried to coax me into involved him exposing his penis to me.

It all started when he was at my house and my mum was out at work. That day, we were playing hide and seek. The boys' bedrooms had bunk beds and I was hiding underneath one of these, not on the bottom bunk. I was lying on my front and he was on the bunk above me. Then I poked my head out and he got off the bed and knelt down beside me.

That was when he exposed his penis to me. He was about 13 or 14 at the time. I can't recall if his penis was flaccid or erect. I do know, though, that I was shocked and bewildered. But what was to follow was even more shocking and incomprehensible.

'Just put this in your mouth,' he said in a matter-of-fact tone, as if he was offering me a sweet.

'What!' I cried in alarm at the idea of this unnatural act. All I knew about the penis was that it was dirty because boys had a wee from it.

He repeatedly said, 'Just do it, it won't hurt.'

I kept saying, 'No. No, I don't want to.'

I was still underneath the bunk bed, lying on my front, and he was still kneeling with his penis exposed, just inches from my face. He kept alternately sweet-talking and badgering me to suck it. His pestering of me continued for about ten minutes.

Then he said something along the lines of 'It'll taste fine, because I'll put toothpaste on it.'

In fact, he wanted me to put the toothpaste on his penis. Being an eight-year-old girl, I didn't know the meaning of it all. I just knew it wasn't right. I wasn't even aware that this was a sexual situation. Eventually, he said he would apply the toothpaste himself and he went and got it, obviously believing that this was the only way he could get me to suck his penis.

The next thing I knew, he had the toothpaste tube in his hand and he had started to coat his penis with it. Obviously, either he'd done it before or his warped mind had worked out that little girls would prefer to suck a penis that tasted of toothpaste.

As he rubbed it in, he extolled the virtues of his toothpaste-coated penis. 'It will taste fine,' he tried to reassure me.

I was still verbally resisting his pleas as I lay on my stomach with my head sticking out, but, although I was a little vulnerable, he didn't get hold of me physically.

At the time I didn't know what masturbation was, but he was masturbating in front of me while continually asking me to suck his penis. He wasn't threatening; there was no air of menace in his voice: it was more like pleading with me.

Then, about 20 minutes after he had first knelt down beside me, it all ended. I think he left the room and I came out from beneath the bunk bed.

Soon afterwards, in the typical way a perpetrator of such crimes acts, he came up to me and asked me not to tell anyone about what had happened. 'Don't tell your mum or dad or anything,' I think he said.

'No, I won't,' I replied innocently. And then he left.

He didn't say why I shouldn't tell Mum and I didn't fully understand the implications of what he had just done, other than that it was dirty. When I was older, of course, I realised what had happened:

my innocence had been taken advantage of by this older boy.

It was some seven years after that day before I divulged the details to anyone. I had been asked to attend a meeting with social services, because I was continually leaving home without my parents' permission. Some might have argued at the time that I had invented the whole thing just to get attention, but I could have thought of better ways than raising such an embarrassing issue, especially as it concerned someone close to my family committing an indecent act in front of me.

In view of what I said about the boy to social services, the police had him in for questioning. I couldn't tell you if they came and arrested him, but I do know that he was in the police station with his solicitor and his mother was present during his interview.

When he was interviewed – and this is only what I heard about a year ago – he just started crying and saying, 'I love Hailey, I would never do anything to hurt her.'

He also sent a text message to Colin about what Huntley did to me. It read: 'I could have killed him after what he did to Hailey. I would never do anything to hurt her.' And in a text message to me he wrote: 'You ripped me to pieces when you said that about me.'

I recall that, in a phone conversation in which I spoke to Mum and Dad about it, I said, 'I'm not going to drag it through the courts. I can't anyway, but obviously the police have decided what they are going to do and what they are not going to do.'

In some text messages he sent, and in particular the one where he writes about what he will do to Huntley, he went on to write: '…she killed me when she said that about me and all this.'

So I put it to him that he should take a lie-detector test. 'I am going to pay for it. I will sit and have mine done. Come on, you want to prove that you are not lying, prove your innocence or whatever. You come with me, you don't have to speak to me if you don't want to; you can go on your own. I will go and have mine done and you go and have yours done.

'I've got nothing to prove, you know,' I added. 'You are saying you want to prove your innocence and you are stating that you never did what you did to me, so go for a lie-detector test.

'I'll pay for it but, boy, you had better have a damn good memory, because I have got a good memory. Because I have got no reason to lie about what happened and I remember it as if it was yesterday. I can remember details, word for word. I bet you don't, because you are the one that is lying about it.

'You know whether I am telling the truth or not. How about you?'

And he said to me, 'I'm not having one of them done. You can't force me to.'

I rejected what he said with, 'Well, that is guilt over and done with then, but I would still go for one, even if you didn't. I would still be prepared to go for one tomorrow.'

I know a lie-detector test is not like a judge and jury examining a case, but I believe that it can prove whether you are lying or not, so I would be happy to go for one to show that I have not just been fantasising about it all.

In early 2004, I got a number of death threats. The person issuing them also spoke to Colin, saying he was this and he was that, and Colin told him, 'Well, listen, mate, you are the one that did this and exposed yourself and did this and that to Hailey.'

After that, the idea was never brought up again, because I think my mother probably mentioned it to him and he would have said something like: 'I am not having one done because I have got nothing to prove.'

I haven't been able to speak with him face-to-face since that conversation, only over the phone or via texts. He had moved away from the area before I had actually left home. As far as I am concerned, the police investigation into my allegation sent a great message of comfort out to any abuser: 'Go home, son, or go to the pub and get yourself a stiff drink.'

And did the police come and see me over the matter? No. Did they interview me? No. Did social services tell me the outcome of the matter? No. No one did.

All I was told was that, if he had done it, the police would have charged him. That is the same scenario as when I raised the allegations against Ian Huntley, years before he killed to satisfy his evil lust. How many more predators are the police going to let slip through their net?

To say the police have failed me is an under-statement. In five years' time, or fifty, the truth will come out. I refused to testify against Huntley in court – my feeling was, why should I help the police out when I felt that they hadn't helped me.

I am in full-blown bereavement at being deprived of police help or even sympathy. Justice, may you rest in peace, because you are dead.

4

A WALKING TIME BOMB

At 11, I was still a doe–eyed, long–haired, sweet and innocent party pop girl. I enjoyed life and had the knack of making new friends. One of these new friends, Katie Webber, was four years older than me. This was a friendship that I would later come to regret, one that led to Huntley's perversions against me.

How this matchless, younger girl–older girl friendship came about was through my elder brother Hayden. He knew Katie's younger brother, James, and I knew James as well. My cousin, another Katie, lived next door to Katie Webber and they were the same age. That connection also helped to bring about the friendship, otherwise I would not have had any reason to become friends with her. Not that I'm blaming my cousin for what subsequently happened.

My cousin Katie used to ask my mum, 'Can I take Hailey up town?' and Mum would always say yes. Because she was friends with Katie Webber, this Katie used to come along as well.

Cousin Katie started mixing in different circles, with new friends, which meant that she didn't spend as much time going to places with Katie Webber. That was the start of Katie Webber and I becoming closer, more like big sister and little sister. I was immersed in our friendship, perhaps because I had no sisters.

Now, instead of my cousin Katie, it was Katie Webber calling by and asking my mum, 'Is it OK if I take Hailey up town shopping?'

Mum used to say, 'There you go, there's some money for a McDonald's or whatever.'

Katie would buy me a Happy Meal with it and then get some fags with the change. I hadn't begun to smoke then. In a way, this was ideal for my mum, as she didn't have to give her time to me.

Each Saturday from then onwards, Katie used to take me to town and I think she used to enjoy taking me because the change that she had left from my meal supplemented her fag money.

I used to go to Katie's house about every other day, so we saw a lot of each other. I lived at number 3 and Katie lived a short walk away up the road. I used to pass her house every day when I went to school, so I felt quite comfortable calling in to see her, and my mum was happy for me to go there, even though she kept a close eye on my movements.

One Saturday, with excitement fluttering around in my stomach about going into town with Katie, I quickly got ready and dressed. I think it was about a quarter to twelve when she came to the house and said to Mum, 'Hiya, Mandy, is it OK if Hailey comes up town with me? We're catching the twelve o'clock bus.'

Mum, of course, said, 'Yes, that's fine, Katie, as long as she's back by five for her tea. Here's some money for a McDonald's.'

As I'd been in a bit of a rush to get ready, my hair wasn't brushed properly. Mum looked at me in utter shock and, as her eyes opened wider, she screamed, 'Actually, Hailey, you are not going anywhere like that. Go and brush your hair. Go on, go upstairs and brush your hair.'

Mum didn't want me going out a bit scruffy, and not wanting to make a scene I said to Katie, 'OK then, I have just got to brush my hair and put my trainers on and then I will be down.'

She said, 'I will just meet you at my house then. See you then. You do your hair.'

Not wanting to delay things, I replied, 'All right then, I'll see you in a minute.'

I was rushing and thinking, I've got to get up to town with Katie for a McDonald's and all of the rest of it. I brushed my hair and I got my shoes on and as I hurried out of the house, I called out, 'See you later, Mum.'

As I rushed out the door, Mum's words trailed off, 'Don't be late…'

I tore along to Katie's and I remember briefly spotting Mrs Webber in her dressing gown, looking out from the bay window of the semi-detached council house. Just before I disappeared from her view, down the drive to the side of the house, towards the caravan that was parked there in front of a big shed, a large bottle of Pepsi caught my eye. A trivial thing, but that's how clear my recall of that day is.

I suppose my senses were heightened as I was in such a hurry to get into town. Katie's gran lived next door to her, and it was a close-knit community, so I'd felt safe enough walking the short distance to my friend's house by myself. And, anyway, I didn't have anything to fear.

Let me explain about that caravan. Because Katie was only 15 at the time and her boyfriend was 23, her parents didn't agree with the relationship, so she had started living in the caravan at the side of the house. She was having a relationship with Ian Huntley – boyfriend and girlfriend. So, when Katie said she would see me at her house, she actually meant the caravan.

Personally, I believe she was infatuated with Huntley. She would say, 'Do you mind if I go to the shops, Ian?'

and 'Can I get you anything? Are you sure? I will only be two minutes. I'll be back. Two minutes, Ian.'

Katie had been with Huntley for about eight months, and at that time, September 1997, I had no reason to feel wary of Huntley. There were no warning signs or anything like that. Little did I know there were allegations against Huntley going back as far as August 1995, when the family of a schoolgirl made an allegation that he had had sex with her. Nor was I aware that in April 1996, after a family reported their concerns to her school, social services became aware of another girl said to be involved with Huntley. The following month two further allegations against Huntley had been reported to social services by the families of other girls. On no occasion was there evidence upon which to prosecute Huntley. They say there is none so blind as those that refuse to see. I say there is none so blind as North East Lincolnshire Social Services and the Humberside Police Force.

As I look back on it, I wonder why no one became suspicious of the goings-on. Had I or anyone else been aware that such a filthy pervert was living in their neighbourhood, perhaps the death of two little girls could have been avoided.

I believe that all sex offenders, and especially those with multiple allegations against them, should be made known to the locality where they live. I am not talking about a one-off charge against someone with no previous convictions or a single allegation in this sphere of crime. I mean someone like Huntley, who was the subject of a number of allegations.

I had not learned anything about Huntley that would have alerted me to what he was. I had no reason, as an 11-year-old girl, to be wary of him. No one said, 'This guy likes to have sex with young girls.'

I was never with Katie's parents enough to get to hear what they thought of him. All I knew was that they didn't like the fact that Katie was not going to school. For by then she had left school of her own accord, and she never went back.

Let me describe Katie. She always had her hair long; it was dark brown and halfway down her back, not as long as mine. It was permed into ringlets and she used to gel, spray and mousse it every morning. She wore make-up and she was paranoid about wearing glasses, which she wore for reading. From what I can remember, she lived in tracksuit bottoms, trousers or jeans. I would say she dressed like a chav.

My opinion on Katie living with a man eight years her senior would be like the pot calling the kettle black. Obviously, because of the situation that I am in now, I can't comment without appearing to be condescending. What I can say is that, although she used to hang about with me, a few years younger than her, she was quite mature for her age. So I never questioned that she was seeing a 23-year-old man.

Mind you, she did brag about it. She would shoot her mouth off and say, 'I get fags and I get beer and if I want this I can have it.'

In Katie's defence, I must add that she would often say that he was always cuddling her and that 'He looks after me' and 'He buys me cigarettes.' As I got older I used to think, Just because he buys you cigarettes, it doesn't mean you have to live with him. If I remember correctly, he stopped buying her things; he stopped buying her beer and pizzas and treating her to things like that. That's just what I noticed; it wasn't anything she told me. In fact, everything she was telling me seemed to be the reverse in real life. So, with that in mind, because she said she was happy with him, then maybe she wasn't at all.

For a while, though, I do think she was happy with him.

I recall how they met. Huntley was working for Katie's mum, Jackie, knocking on doors and selling raffle tickets for a child support charity. Sir Christopher Kelly's report, mentioned in the Introduction to this book, suggested that Katie's relationship with Huntley started as early as 1995.

My brother Hayden's friendship with James Webber would be the catalyst for a fateful and accidental meeting between me and the future Soham killer Ian Huntley. And, as I said, no one in the community, as far as I know, raised an eyebrow about him living there in that caravan with a girl of 15. But he was a walking time bomb, waiting to go off.

5

WE CAN DO IT THE EASY WAY
OR THE HARD WAY

THE SKY WAS BABY BLUE WITH JUST A HINT OF WISPY CLOUD, THERE WAS A WARM BREEZE AND THE LAST RAYS OF THE SUMMER SUN WERE SHINING BRIGHTLY. A perfect day for a trip into town, filled with excitement for a young girl: a mixture of McDonald's and window shopping.

I was wearing my brother's tracksuit bottoms, tied around the waist with a cord-type pull fastener, a T-shirt with a fleecy jumper on top of it and a tracksuit top over that, and Nike trainers.

As I walked up the drive to the caravan, a thrill surged within me at what lay ahead that day. I expected Katie to be waiting for me inside, and I was about to knock on the door when I spotted Huntley through the caravan window, sitting alone at the table. As I stood there momentarily, waiting for Katie to come out, I caught the faintest aroma of freshly cut grass, carried on the gentle remnants of the breeze.

I was pulled out of my world of serenity by Huntley's soft voice drifting through the wafer-thin door. 'Come in,' he called out, as he motioned with his arm from behind the picture-postcard window for me to enter.

As I went in he greeted me warmly, 'Hi.'

'Is Katie here?' I asked.

Huntley was no stranger to me; we had previously met and spoken. I had no idea of his past, and no one had told me to mind him. To me, he was Katie Webber's boyfriend. But, to fill out the picture, it was only because I had won my mum's trust about my flourishing friendship with Katie that I was allowed to call and see her in the caravan she shared with her boyfriend.

'No, she's just nipped out to the shop,' Huntley casually replied to my question. 'She'll only be ten or fifteen minutes or so.'

Having known Huntley for a few months, and because he was known to my mum and dad, I was completely at ease as I entered the chintzy caravan to wait for my friend. All the same, I tried to cover my awkward feeling of self-consciousness at finding Katie wasn't there by saying, 'Oh, I was supposed to go to town with her today. I don't know what's happened there then. It must be confusion or crossed wires.'

What I can't fully work out, when I look back, is why didn't Katie return home directly from my place? Because, when she had called by earlier and I wasn't ready, she said we'd meet at the caravan. And how could Huntley be so certain that she would be back in such a short time as he said, since, as far as he knew, Katie had planned to be in town all afternoon with me. Surely she had told him that this was what we were doing, or had she just told him she was popping out for a short while? If so, why would she have told him a lie like this?

After a while the subject changed and Huntley rather cleverly made a comment that was his key to the door into a far deeper conversation. 'Oh well, you're not allowed to leave the street on your own, are you?' he said.

Without giving a moment's heed to any ulterior motive behind his question, I replied, 'No.'

'Oh, well, why can't you leave the street on your own then?' he pressed me.

I had no reason to be cautious over his motive for asking these questions as I replied, 'Because my mum says that I am not allowed to,' quickly adding, 'I think I maybe got it wrong. I can only leave the street with an adult.'

Little did I realise from Huntley's calm demeanour what he had in store for me; nothing crossed my 11-year-old mind. The table, which could be folded down into a bed, had pornographic magazines fanned out on it; the pages were spread open, revealing naked models that Huntley had clearly been ogling.

During the course of this conversation that Huntley had initiated, he emphasised how careful my mum was about me. 'Your mum's really strict; she doesn't let you out of the street, does she?'

'Yeah, because I want to go and buy sweets,' I innocently replied.

Already Huntley was aware of how my mum kept a watchful eye on me. She strictly supervised my movements and I might as well have been tagged – that's how much I was monitored.

The malevolent mind of this man was now steering the conversation his way as he said soothingly, 'Your mum's *really* strict, just like mine was. I was never allowed to do anything.'

We were still talking about my leaving the street when Huntley orchestrated a question that would turn the metaphorical key already in the door of innocence. He took his eyes off the girlie magazines, looked straight at me with his deep, fiery eyes and out of the blue asked, 'What's the most daring thing you've done with a boy?'

That was the first time I felt uncomfortable and a bit out of place in his presence. In a way, looking back on it, he dared me to reveal my innermost thoughts. It was as if he was challenging all the boundaries with his invitation to reveal to him what little I could about my experiences with boys.

With wide-eyed innocence, I looked back at

Huntley's unlocking eyes and asked, 'Well, what do you mean about *daring?*'

With his disarming manner, he prompted me with an example. 'Have you kissed boys, sort of thing?'

Embarrassed and with an uncomfortable shrug of my shoulders, I replied, 'No, no. But I've played kiss-chase around the school playground.'

This revelation, that I had kissed a boy, although just in a game, was something that I wouldn't have wanted even my mum to find out about.

Huntley was moving in on his victim: me. Huntley wasn't your 'abduct and assault' paedophile. Exerting control, for him, was a gradual process and the start of that process was his pushing at the door of opportunity by saying to me, 'I'll tell you what, Hailey, why don't we go for a walk? And we can climb some trees, because you've had a really boring life like me.'

Alarm bells started ringing in my head about how Mum would go mad if I disobeyed her, so I replied defensively, 'Well, I'm not allowed out of the end of the street!'

Huntley deftly defused my reply with his charm. 'Well, you said earlier that you were allowed out of the street with an adult.' And then he pushed further, 'Aren't you?'

'Yeah,' I replied.

The boundaries of safety and the protective custody of the street were being whittled away by Huntley's accelerated grooming of me so as to get me out of the street and to some secluded spot where he could carry out his sick wishes. He was talking to me as if we were both 11 years old when he pulled me into his make-believe world by revealing, 'My mum, when I was your age, she was really strict, she wouldn't let me do anything, and it's so unfair, isn't it?'

'Well, yes,' I had to agree.

All through our conversation I was sitting across the table from him. He was still, from time to time, gazing intently at the magazines. He didn't make any effort to conceal this from me; he had this particular one right open in front of him.

It was a Saturday and, by the look of him, he had decided it was a rest day, as I recall him having stubble on his chin; he was dressed in a T-shirt that was tucked into his jeans and he wore flat scruffy work shoes.

I remember looking at his hair and thinking, God, you're not that much older than me. Although he had jet-black hair, there were sizeable grey streaks running through it. This gave me the impression that he was already turning grey. He had mucky hands. He didn't have aftershave on; he didn't use a body spray either.

When I went into the caravan that Saturday, there was dog hair everywhere and the musty smell of wet fur. Huntley had an Alsatian puppy called Sadie. It was the one Maxine Carr went on to keep after she was released from her prison sentence for giving him his false alibi over the Soham murders.

Huntley then skilfully referred again to my life in the street, saying, 'You've a bit of a boring life, haven't you? Your mum is really strict and so is your dad. They don't let you go out of the street.'

Then, cunningly, he threw a searching look at me as he probed further about what he had already touched on. 'Have you ever climbed trees?'

Knowing how angry my mum would be if she caught me doing that, I warily replied, 'No. I'm not allowed to climb trees.'

Returning to another of his themes, he said, 'God, you've had a bit of a boring life, haven't you, kid?'

'Well, yeah. Yeah,' I replied nonchalantly.

'Yeah, and you wouldn't climb a tree, you say?' Huntley quizzed me. 'It's not the kind of thing that you would do?'

'No.'

'Or not allowed to do, rather?'

'No, because my mum always said, "You climb trees, you fall and break your neck."'

'Yes, you've had a really boring life, haven't you?' he said, pressing his earlier point.

'Well, it's a bit unfair that I'm not allowed out of the street without an adult. All my friends are allowed out of the street. Even to go to the corner shop, I'd have to have an adult with me.'

It was true. I was only allowed out on my own in our street, where my mum could walk out of her front door, look left – 'She's not down there' – look right – 'Oh, she's down that end' – and then she could call me in.

So that was when Huntley beguilingly said, 'Well, *I'm* an adult. Why don't you go out of the street with *me* and we'll go and climb some trees. Your mum knows me and so does your dad.'

When I look back on it now, it was in a really charming – how can I put it? – a smooth-talking, befriending sort of way that he then said, 'We'll go out of the street, we'll go and climb some trees and, you know, it's all right because I'm an adult and you'll be fine.'

'Oh, yeah,' I gushed, 'Mum and Dad know you and my auntie Sue lives next door and my cousin Katie lives next door and Mum knows Jackie, Katie Webber's mum, and, oh yeah, OK then. OK.'

Using that as his cue, Huntley folding his magazine once and then again, before stuffing it down the side of his seat. Then, beaming a smile at me, he repeated reassuringly, 'Your mum and dad know me. *I'm* an adult, it'll be fine.'

The trap was set for me when I thought for a lingering moment that what he was saying was right. And that's when the rebel in me accepted his offer with gusto. 'All right then,' I answered.

Off we went, step by step, the safe confines of my

street disappearing into the distance. Huntley led the way in what, to him, was a walk of lustful abandonment. He must have been preoccupied with the wicked thoughts of what he wanted to do to me running around inside his head. Knowing what I now know about Huntley, this is probably what he had done to the Soham girls, Holly and Jessica, before murdering them.

I recall that, as we walked past the window of Katie's house, her mum Jackie wasn't there. She wasn't by the window, as she had been when I arrived. We walked out of the sanctuary of the street, ambled through this alleyway that I used to walk through every morning on the way to school and then we went across a road before trekking through the grounds of my school – Huntley always leading the way, with me keenly following close behind.

We were generally talking about school and where Katie had got to, and he was reassuring, saying, 'I wonder where she could have got to? Don't worry, I'll tell her you were looking for her.'

Picturing trees in my mind, I replied cheerfully, 'Oh, don't worry.'

We were as talkative as each other. You couldn't shut me up; I could have talked the head off a brush. This was going to be much better than a day in town. Climbing trees would make this a great Saturday. It was like going from felt to velvet.

We walked for over 30 minutes, at about three to four miles an hour, which means it must have been a mile and half to two miles from the caravan. I didn't know where we were going, and he never said where he was taking me. I just assumed we were going to climb trees.

Huntley had done a good job in not arousing any suspicion in me about what he had planned in his brooding mind. It was as if he was an old hand at this.

I blindly followed where Huntley led. We made our way through the school grounds, towards and then across the playing field. There was the main entrance, but we didn't walk that way, we walked right across the far side of the field, where there was an open walkway.

As we passed my school, the scheming Huntley lured me deeper into his trap, exploiting the false sense of security he had already created within me. After spotting some trees, he gawped at them, chuckled and said, 'Oh, them bloody trees are no good.'

After all, what would a little girl of 11 think was wrong with a grown man of 23 wanting to climb trees?

Then, as we got across the other side of the field, where there were houses, we followed a series of winding roads. We ended up at the Grosvenor pub, in Cleethorpes, where people were gathered outside having a drink. There were wooden benches with people sitting on them, and many more drinkers standing about with beer glasses in their hands. I can remember thinking that I was thirsty, but I didn't say anything to Huntley, as I didn't want to delay our tree-climbing expedition.

We passed through the mass of people milling about in the garden, round the side of the pub and to a fence at the far side of the car park. Huntley beckoned me through a gap in the fence and, behind it, in contrast to the other, bustling side, was a secluded orchard, like a secret garden. We two were the only ones there, although it seemed to be part of the pub's grounds.

The thickly wooded area that greeted us was not at all frightening or displeasing to the eye. Ferns sprouted from the shaded areas beneath the moss-covered trees, their leaves fanning out in a welcoming wave of green tasselled arms. Looking like a picture postcard, sporadic clumps of dense bracken fused together with dead wood and leaves, as brambles battled their way through to reach the light. Beneath the aged branches of the trees, where the wind had blown the bullion from them, lay a carpet of golden leaves, strewn across the untouched ground. As we walked, twigs broke beneath our feet, making cracking noises before being silenced by the spongy earth.

Huntley looked at me and prompted, 'Go and pick a tree.'

Swept along by his charm, I struggled to contain my excitement and eagerly pointed to an octopus-limbed tree by the fence at the far end of the orchard. 'All right then, what about that one?' I said, seeking his approval.

'You won't be able to climb that,' he challenged me with a chuckle.

'I will, I will,' I insisted.

He looked at me in astonishment, then gasped cheerfully, 'Do you think you will?'

'Yes. All right then,' I said confidently.

I scampered through the wild undergrowth, got my foot up on the fence behind the tree and clambered up on to one of its branches. Just as I was reaching out for a more secure hold, waves of shock and fear swept through my body as I became aware of Huntley's mucky, searching hands grasping my waist roughly and with some force. I knew something was not quite right; this wasn't a friendly hand helping me up the tree. For some inexplicable reason, I was paralysed with fear. Although I didn't swear, I knew what it was, and in that fleeting moment I thought, Oh, no! Shit, I mean, what's all this about? I shouldn't have come here.

My survival instinct kicked in, warning me something was wrong. I didn't know what it was, but the feeling was uncomfortable and not one I was used to. In that split second, as I held on to the safety of the friendly-looking tree, wide-eyed panic took over as Huntley's grubby fingers blindly and wildly groped me in places they should never have been.

I looked around at him in abject horror and I asked, 'What's the matter?'

With ease, he spun me around towards him, away

from the last vestiges of safety offered by the branch I
was clinging to. As my hands slithered off the branch
and I faced him, his eyes pierced deep into mine.
Instantly, I was transfixed, and then he took me by
surprise when he said something like, 'It's you that I
love. I don't love Katie.'

The harmless look he had in his eyes when he was in
the caravan had been consumed with what I would
now call a sinister, brooding look of lust. His whole
expression had transformed into something no longer
recognisable as the Huntley I knew: his eyes were lit up
and his mouth had got wider. It was what I would
describe as a crazed look; yes, that is the word. Looking
back on it now, it was as if he was on some kind of
drugs. His eyes were really wide open and his whole
face had become fused and distorted with anger. I
remember feeling scared seeing this man with the look
of a gargoyle about him.

Without me realising or being able to react against it,
Huntley had me firmly wedged between him and the
trunk of the tree. He dropped his hands to his sides, as
if to signify that I had to stand there and face him.

Huntley dwarfed me as he defiantly stared down at
me. Yet, strangely enough, I remember the soft, golden
rays of the sun shining through the soft leaves of the
trees, casting shadows across what was, seconds earlier, a
vision of unspoiled beauty. The image in my mind of
what I'd thought was the Garden of Eden was now

gone. Suddenly the place looked like a menacing, wild and mouldering orchard.

I had to squint against the constantly changing shafts of sunlight that shone though the aged, softly swaying branches. Peering at him, I saw Huntley had changed from being my happy-go-lucky tree-climbing pal to a silhouetted spectre of evil.

I felt really uneasy as he ran his searching fingers through my hair. With each stroke of his hand, he was cooing incoherently. It was like lightning striking me.

Wide-eyed with disbelief, I cried out, 'What are you doing?'

As Huntley panted, his stinking breath sending shivers of revulsion shooting down my spine, he told me, 'It's you I want. I don't want Katie.'

Not grasping what he meant, I asked, 'What do you mean?'

'Come on, Hailey, I really love you,' he coaxed, his eyes glazed. 'It's you I want. I don't want Katie. I really love you!'

Shaken, I told him, 'You love Katie, you don't love me.'

By now I was in a blind panic about what he was going to do. Looking back, I can see how far he had become detached from reality as he continued his barrage of crazy words.

I had really long, brown hair that hung right down my back like silk, and, as he kept pawing it with his clammy, smelly hand, he spurted a torrent of half-incomprehensible words that had my insides reeling in even more shock. 'Katie cut her hair off, I wish she hadn't.' And he kept saying over and over again, 'I don't love Katie, I love you, I love your hair.'

'No! Please, Ian, don't!' I pleaded.

Huntley's lustful and perverted words were lost on me, they meant nothing to me, but something was about to happen that would haunt me for the rest of my life.

As Huntley pawed me, he said something that sent waves of fear through my body, 'It won't hurt.'

And then, as he looked at me with cold, unfeeling eyes, he repeated, 'I really love you. I don't love Katie, she's disgusting, she makes my stomach churn. She's cut all her hair off, because it was long and permed and then she went and had it cut. I don't like it. Your hair is beautiful. Keep your hair long for me, won't you? Oh, it's fantastic.' And he just kept going on like this.

All I kept thinking was, I shouldn't have come here. I knew I shouldn't have gone out of the street. That is what Mum used to tell me all the time, 'Don't go out of the street, don't go out of the street,' and I shouldn't have done, because of what was happening now.

My nerves were in chaos. I didn't know what his intentions were, what it was all leading to. All I could think was, How can he say he loves me when he's going out with Katie, my best friend?

As his eyes locked with mine, he held my gaze and angrily spat, 'Stuff Katie. I don't love her, you're the one that I love.'

I was getting even more scared, and pressed him, 'Can we go home now?'

His eyes had become even more fierce and powerful, and as he held my gaze further he fired at me, 'No, not until you've listened to what I've got to say first.'

Then, clearly deciding actions spoke louder than words, he wanted me to undo my tracksuit trousers. The tone of his voice changed to something more disturbing as he demanded in a harsher tone, 'Undo your toggle on your tracksuit bottoms.'

The crude words that followed were alien to me. 'I want to finger you.'

'What's that?' I asked, truly confused.

His eyes were now even more ablaze with madness than they had been and his face was hideously contorted when he ordered, 'Just let me do it.'

'No, please,' I cried.

Blind lust was leading him on as he growled, 'No, just let me do it.'

I begged him not to do something I didn't know the meaning of, though I knew from his demeanour and the tone of his voice that it was bad. 'No, I don't want you to,' I pleaded.

Repulsed by his foul breath, I pulled back a bit and I felt the coarse, moss-covered bark of the tree pressing against the back of my head. I tried to reason with him, 'You don't love me, you have got to love Katie. You're living with Katie. She loves you and she thinks of you first of all.'

This only set off another torrent of demanding words. He kept pleading, 'Come on, just let me do it,' clearly intent on wearing down my resistance verbally.

But then, although he didn't force himself on me, his hands started to wander over me again and his breathing became deeper and faster. In this secluded place, one that Huntley obviously knew well, I knew I was in a very menacing situation.

The reasons he gave for why I should let him 'finger' me were nothing but accelerated cultivation of a victim – exactly as I now suspect he tried with Jessica Chapman and Holly Wells before killing them. I believe that they, like me, resisted their little hearts out before Huntley snapped, carried out his evil deeds and then killed them. All while Maxine Carr was away visiting relatives in Grimsby.

With a new-found smugness to his voice, he kept saying, 'It won't hurt. Trust me, it won't hurt. Just let me do it to you.'

I went on pleading with him, 'No, no, no.' I was now crying as I begged, 'Please, Ian. I'm scared.'

Somehow I managed to extricate myself from his wandering hands and repulsive breath. I sidestepped away from the tree and then backwards. As I edged away from Huntley, I was crying again. In an effort to stop him from groping me, I knelt down in a protective posture. I remember feeling the coldness of the earth, in comparison to the warmth of the sun, seeping into the knees of my tracksuit bottoms as I implored, 'Please, Ian, no!'

I dropped into the kneeling position because I didn't want Huntley to undo my tracksuit bottoms, as he was now groping between my legs. I was just a young girl, I didn't know about the sexual role of the vagina; to me, it was for urinating. Please, I was thinking, don't make me undo my trousers. If I'm kneeling down, he can't undo them.

I thought that was fine until he ordered, 'Stand up and talk to me.'

I just put my head in my hands and started crying uncontrollably and shaking with fear. All the while he was running his hands over my hair.

The only defensive thing I could do was to pull my head away from his hands as I repeated again and again, 'Please, don't. I just want to go home, Ian.'

'No, no, no,' he shouted at me. 'You're fine with me, you're fine. You're safe here. Nothing will happen, you're safe. Just do as I say and you'll be fine.'

As soon as he said that I thought, What do you mean, *as long as I do as you say, I will be fine?* Oh, God. I shouldn't be here, I kept thinking. I knew I shouldn't be out of the street.

'Please,' I cried, trying to be calmer, 'I'm going to be late home for my tea. Please.'

'No. No, you can stay with me,' he insisted, and we went on and on like this, I would say for about an hour.

I was still on my knees, crying torrents and pleading as he continued to paw at my now dishevelled hair. Eventually, I did what he asked and stood up. From where I stood I could see the gate leading out of the orchard and a blue plastic sheet in the shape of an igloo that looked as though tiny kids could crawl underneath it.

I kept this blue shape in view as I tried to inch away from Huntley, and all the time crazy thoughts were running through my head. Should I just run away? No, I can't, he can run quicker than me, I bet, and I won't be able to get to the gate. There is no way out.

I remember the stillness being disturbed by the *brrrrrr-brrrrrr* of pneumatic drills. Workmen were drilling the road right behind me, beyond the back of the orchard. I could hear them shouting. I couldn't make out what they were saying, but I could hear the noise of their shouts despite the drilling.

We had been there for at least an hour, and all I could think was, I don't want him to put his hands down my trousers, I just want to go home. If Mum finds out I've left the street and I'm not home by about four or five o'clock, I'm going to be in big trouble.

Huntley kept cajoling and badgering me as he

growled with lust, 'You know, just let me put my hands in your trousers and do this to you. It won't hurt, trust me, it will not hurt.'

'I just want to go home,' I kept on begging him.

The faces of those close to me flashed before my eyes as I suddenly realised what being at home was all about. I just kept crying, 'I'm scared and I want to go home; people will know that I am with you.'

At one point, I thought that being trapped here like this was going to be my life – held prisoner here for ever. I remember the fir trees. I was just staring at them and thinking, I don't want to look at him because he's too scary to look at. When I did look, his face had become even more unrecognisable, vile and contorted than ever.

I gripped the top of my trousers as if my life depended on it and, looking back to that day, maybe it did. After a while my fingers hurt and, as my strength waned, I thought, God, please!

With tears of utter despair running down my cheeks, I sobbed uncontrollably, 'It's going to hurt.'

Huntley snapped, 'No, it won't hurt, it won't hurt,' and then, as suddenly as it had started, it stopped.

He had become the epitome of what I now understand paedophilia to be all about. He had come of paedophilic age and here he was having his own evil rites of passage by putting his hands down my trousers.

As bizarre as it may sound, my biggest fear of all was

still that Mum would tell me off for leaving our street without her permission. This was more of a concern than Huntley actually making his alien demands to 'finger' me. I didn't think he would actually do whatever it was, and then, obviously, I discovered what 'fingering' was.

I was still begging Huntley, 'Please, can I go home.'

My resolve and fortitude were already broken enough by what had happened over that terrible hour. But what now emanated from Huntley's vile mouth sent a sadness reverberating through me that would have broken the heart of anyone who witnessed my suffering; but there were only the two of us there.

My jaw dropped and my soul seemed to be smashed into a million pieces as Huntley finally cracked and the darker side of him manifested itself as something truly demonic and he spat, 'Listen, bitch, let me do it again, otherwise I'll kill you!'

As I searched his eyes for an ounce of compassion, all I could see were a thousand wicked thoughts in the windows of his soul as I implored, 'Oh no, please!'

This was no longer just about escaping from Huntley to get home to an irate and worried mother: this was now about my life! The sexual appetite that had shadowed him for all his adult life had finally burst out, and he threatened me, 'Right, we can do it the easy way or the hard way.'

'What's the easy way?' I asked fearfully.

In what to me now was a precursor to the murders of Holly and Jessica, Huntley seethed as he poured out his desire to inflict pain on me. 'The easy way is for me to press just behind your ears, because I'm a black belt in karate.'

In a burst of dry tears, I blubbered at him, 'What will that do?'

With an air of chilling menace, Huntley hurriedly spoke his instructions. 'All you will do, right, is either pass out or black out for five or ten minutes. Let me do what I want to do to you and then you will wake up and you will be fine.'

'If that's the easy way,' I asked, 'what's the hard way? Because I might die if you press there. What happens if you don't mean to kill me but I don't wake up?'

Huntley seemed to think he was giving me a choice when, in fact, the option was either to succumb to being blacked out or to carry on struggling. Then, after a short time, he rasped, 'The hard way is, if you *don't* fucking let me do it, I will put my fingers there anyway, and I will press real hard there. And if I press so hard, you *will* die and I *will* do what I want to do to you anyway!'

On hearing what was likely to happen to me, I unleashed a stream of tears, along with a heart-rending plea, 'Please, I just want to go home. I don't want you to do it, please. I just want to go home.'

Little by little, I was backing away from him towards

the fence, but he was still only feet away from me. It seemed that, for every step back I took, he inched closer towards me in this continuing bizarre dance of the predator and his prey. As he did so, he leaned forward, stooping over me. He was breaching the invisible barrier around me, the barrier we all have around us. Once more I was feeling very uncomfortable, yet I was powerless to stop him.

Huntley was inches away from me and my skin crawled. I renewed my grip on my tracksuit bottoms. I was becoming increasingly scared because he kept putting his hand near my neck. I was frantically thinking, He's just going to press it or something and I'm going to drop dead. I didn't know what happened if someone pressed behind your ears, and he was trying to do that to me.

When you get cold or you see something eerie, the hairs on the back of your neck stand on end. Well, that's how I would feel for another hour, as I kept up my unrelenting plea to be allowed to go home.

Huntley had gone from feigning putting his hands behind my ears to slowly running his fingers through my hair again, and each time his hand passed my ear I would let out an audible gasp as I thought, He's going to kill me. At that time I thought someone just had to press the area and you would drop down dead. With every terrifying pass of his hand, I thought I was in the shadow of death. Fear swept through me each time and

I would pull my head away from his evil touch. I remember thinking, Don't touch it there, because I might die. It had stuck in my head when he said I could die if he pressed just a bit too hard.

I remember feeling a bit queasy as I rasped again, 'Oh, please, Ian, I just want to go home; my mum is going to kill me. I'm going to be late for my tea and she knows that I'm going to be with you. Please, just let me go home.'

And then a determined look came across his face and, without any hesitation, he moved my hands away and did it to me again: he pushed his fingers into my vagina. He actually made contact with it from inside my tracksuit bottoms. He had been gripping the top of my trousers and forcing them into my belly. I didn't know these invasive procedures were all just so that he could have his moment of glory.

In his state of excitement, he gulped down air and kept growling, 'Move your hands away, move your hands away.'

All the while I kept on begging him, 'Oh, please. Please, Ian, don't. It's going to hurt. Please, no.'

Without an ounce of compassion he kept going, telling me, 'No, it's not going to hurt. Just let me do it.'

I was wailing now, 'Please, Ian, don't. I'm going to be late home and I have got to go home for tea.'

If I kept saying that, he might let me go, I thought. I knew what he was trying to do was wrong. I didn't know what the details of the wrongness of it were, but I knew instinctively that something was wrong about it because *nothing like this* had ever happened to me before. And I didn't know when, if or how it was going to end.

By now Huntley's hand was crawling around inside my knickers and it made contact with my flesh again. In total he did it about four or five times. Every time he inserted his fingers into my private parts, he stopped and pulled away a little bit when I started crying, 'Please, stop it, it's hurting me.'

Then his manner became cajoling. 'Don't be silly. Don't be silly.'

I noticed now that, when I started crying, he pulled away and stopped doing it for a while. Then I dried my eyes, tried to gather myself and started hoping and praying that he might let me go home in a minute. No sooner had I thought that then he started the cycle all over again and then I started crying and he pulled away a little bit and he would stop. Each time he fingered my vagina, it went on for up to five minutes. During the attack and afterwards he repeatedly mentioned putting his fingers behind my ears and pressing.

Then, after he had done the same sexual act to me yet again, I managed to stand up on the bottom ledge of the fence and I looked over and started screaming to the men drilling the road, 'Help me.'

I was waving one arm frantically because Huntley

was holding the other. And I was yelling in blind panic, 'Please, help me. Come over here!' It was then that I realised my cries were falling on literally deaf ears, as the guys drilling the road were wearing ear defenders. I think they were yellow or red.

I could see lots of workmen, but they couldn't hear my calls or see my arm waving desperately. That was when Huntley put his hands around my waist and pulled me down out of sight of anyone on the other side of the fence. Then he undid my trousers again and carried out another sexual assault, the same as before. He was still in a state of arousal, although he hadn't exposed himself to me.

With the clatter of the pneumatic drills, I couldn't hear the babble coming out of Huntley's mouth; I could just see his lips moving. As he drew closer to me, my head was in bits, but I remember the sickly smell of his breath, diluted a little by my own heavy, anxious breathing.

Looking back, the odd thing is that Huntley didn't expose his penis or fondle himself. What he was doing to me was a perverse thing for his own mental gratification. This was maybe something he would run through his head at another time; perhaps even now when he is behind bars. There was no physical gratification for him, other than the pleasure of abusing me. He was deriving a feeling of power from the control he exerted over me. He was feeding himself what he most needed, that sense of power, and getting off on it.

Not long after that, he finally agreed to let me go home. I don't know if this was because I told him I had arranged to meet my mum at the pub that we were behind, but, as I look back on it now, I have the feeling that it might have been entirely due to Huntley's lust having been sated, rather than a response to my constant sobbing and pleading.

When we eventually walked out of the orchard, he threatened me when he raised the subject I was already worried about. 'Well, you can go home but, if you tell anybody, I'll kill you.'

I was petrified and barely managed to stammer my reply, 'No, no. No, I won't. I won't tell anyone. I promise.'

Of course, my reasons for not wanting to tell anyone about what Huntley had done to me were entirely different from how he saw it. Obviously, he wanted to avoid being put behind bars. I wanted to avoid my mum finding out that I had disobeyed her strict orders not to leave the street without first letting her know or getting her permission to do so.

I remember with exhausted relief the feeling of liberation that ran through me as I walked out of the orchard. If I can get back home in time, I thought, I won't have to face a scolding from Mum for leaving the sanctuary of the street. But what if, while Huntley was abusing me, Katie Webber had called at my home to see where I was for our planned visit into town? Mum's rage didn't bear thinking about! My head was in pieces, but I was distracted from my thoughts as I noticed how empty the place was; the crowd of drinkers from two hours earlier had dispersed.

As we retraced our steps back the way we'd come, I was in such a state of severe shock that I said very little. The madness in Huntley's eyes had melted away; the cruel-looking predator of minutes earlier was now looking more like his former self. At that point, I was able to think a little more clearly, and my thoughts were of my mum frantically looking left and right down the street for me.

I was startled out of this dismal vision by the sound of Huntley's voice repeating what he had said earlier, this time his voice more pleading than demanding, 'Don't tell anybody; make sure you don't speak to anybody about it.'

Because of his earlier threat to kill me, I promised again not to tell anyone. Although I was out in the open again, that threat hung over me like a widow's veil.

We carried on walking and arrived back at the field near the school grounds, where I spotted something that gave me hope. It was an old Vauxhall Cavalier, or at least that sort of shape of car. I thought it was the caretaker's and all sorts of jumbled and muddled thoughts ran through my mind. What made me think it was the caretaker's car was because he was often at the school tidying up on a Saturday.

At the thought of this, my muggy head began to clear even more, my eyesight, blurred from crying, began to improve and my survival instinct was kicking in. Halfway across the field I made my move. I ran into the school grounds, leaving Huntley standing there.

In retrospect, knowing what happened to Holly and Jessica when Huntley was a school caretaker, cold shivers of panic run up and down my spine every time I think about how I made a run for it across that field of hope. I believe that my survival may have caused Huntley to murder Holly and Jessica. He knew that they could promise him all he wanted, but that in the end they would do as I had done... escape and eventually tell of what happened.

I was just one witness against Huntley, but Holly and Jessica were two witnesses. He knew that, if they escaped his evil clutches, all would be made known to the police. In exactly the same way as I went knocking on his caravan door, they too went calling on him like lambs to the slaughter. It was as though the sick-minded Huntley was gifted all three of us for his own perverse pleasure.

After a short sprint, I reached what was known as the school's 'quiet area', where there was a tranquil pond for schoolchildren to sit beside. In desperation I looked around for the caretaker, but he wasn't in sight. However, it dawned on me that there were some CCTV cameras around the school that would save me.

By now Huntley, as quick as a greyhound, had dashed after me and was on my tracks!

Near by were the doors to the gym, so I ran there, but I ended up doing a bad job at hiding. The best I could do was just stand near the doors, puffing and panting and shaking with fright. If that wasn't bad enough, the fear of God ran through me as I heard Huntley's ruthless voice booming out, and it was getting worryingly closer. The caretaker has got to be around here somewhere, I told myself in desperation.

'Fucking come here!' Huntley yelled.

When he cornered me, I dared to give him a fleeting glance and, sure enough, what I suspected had happened. The calm demeanour that had briefly returned had now vanished and his face was devoid of any compassion. His evil persona had resurfaced. Maybe my darting away had set him off. Maybe I should have kept the calm demeanour of a lost and helpless girl about me. I don't know.

Now Huntley's fury was increased tenfold. I had dared to defy the control he was obsessed with and this time his eyes had more of a faraway look about them than the crazy look of earlier. His face, darkly friendly at times, had become a brooding mask of malevolence and brutality as he announced loudly and coldly, 'Now I'm going to do it to you again.'

The thought of death once more flashed before my eyes. As the nightmare at his hands in the orchard came flooding back to me, again I found myself begging, 'No, Ian, please don't. Please don't.'

I grasped at one final straw of hope that I might bring Huntley back from the brink when I warned him, 'There are CCTV cameras watching you. Don't!'

As he looked about him, he shattered any hope I had of escape by hissing, 'Oh, don't worry about it, they're fake. They're not real.'

There were quite a few cameras, pointing outwards from the classroom, directly at us, but he didn't care: he was too much in the grip of sexual desire to give a second thought to the consequences. I think that, even if someone had come across him while he was in that state, he would have continued to pursue what he wanted.

'Please, Ian, just let me go home,' I cried out.

Earlier, in the orchard, my screams seemed to work, but now they were useless. Deaf to my begging and pleading, he sexually assaulted me yet again.

My rainbow thoughts of being tucked up in the warmth of my bed were soon snow-covered and I started to cry again. He seemed to be regaining some grip of himself when he told me to stop, but I had a lump in my throat and I was finding it hard to bring it to an end. My eyes were red and started stinging. After so much crying there were hardly any tears left.

Any hopes I had of Huntley ceasing his attack on me were shattered when he said, 'This is the last time that I will do it to you.'

It was a prospect that I had been barely able to imagine a few moments earlier, and it brought mixed feelings of relief and revulsion.

But then, as his hands roved over my body, he calmly demanded, 'Just let me do it one more time.'

I weakly croaked, 'Oh, please. No!'

Regardless of my pleading and trying to reason with him, he went berserk and continued to stoke up his lust by forcing his fingers inside my most intimate place.

By this time, he had me pushed up against the gym door with his forearm and pressed his body against me, and he wanted to do it again and again and again.

Desperate, I pointed again and cried out, 'There are video cameras there. Don't do it.'

But Huntley, by now wildly aroused and unstoppable, shouted breathlessly, 'They're fake, they don't work.'

The physical and mental torture for me was nearly over when, awkwardly, he withdrew his hand from my tracksuit bottoms and his eyes darted about to see if we were still alone. Maybe now that he was out of his sexual stupor, the cameras worried him.

He again threatened, 'If you run, I'll come after you! If you dare to tell anybody, then I'll come and kill you. Just remember, Hailey, I only live down the street from you,' he rasped, 'and I'm a black belt in karate!'

He scared the living daylights out of me, and out of fear I promised once again, 'No, I won't tell anyone. I promise, I won't say anything to anyone.'

We set off again and, on the last leg of the walk home, he drilled it into my head: 'If you tell anybody, I'll come and kill you.'

I was devastated at the thought of not reaching home and promised yet again to tell no one.

When my street came into sight I had to stifle sobs of joy as I thought, Thank God!

And at the same time I was consumed with the chill of death as I thought of Huntley's threats to murder me.

Then he left my side, without saying a word, and went into the driveway of Katie Webber's house, where the caravan was.

Just in case he had changed his mind and was coming after me to kill me, I gave a worried glance over my shoulder as I started walking faster. When he left my sight, I wasn't aware if Katie was there... I was just pleased to be alive and back in the street.

6

WASHING AWAY THE DEMONS

I REMEMBER TREMBLING WITH RELIEF WHEN, A FEW HOUSES AWAY FROM MINE, THE AROMA OF SPAGHETTI BOLOGNESE WAS CARRIED TOWARDS ME ON THE SAME GENTLE SUMMER BREEZE THAT HAD BROUGHT ME THE SMELL OF GRASS CUTTINGS A FEW HOURS EARLIER. That homely smell was coming from my house. I remember knocking on the outer door and then my mum saw me through the glass of the inner one. 'Hang on, my spaghetti might burn,' she shouted.

Crying had given me puffy-looking eyes, and they felt like organ stops, but in the time it took to walk home from the school they had become less inflamed. Quickly, I tidied up my clothes and hair. Mum didn't give me a second glance, and why should she, for as far as she was concerned I had been into town with Katie Webber. I never let on what had happened. Besides, Mum never paid much attention to me when I came home; it was when I was going out that I had to be careful to always look my best, or she would nag me.

I had been so scared of the consequences of having left the street, and now here I was back home, with Mum none the wiser.

As I was undressing to take a bath, I noticed bleeding. I hadn't started my periods at this age, so I wasn't aware of what menstrual blood was. And, anyway, looking back, this certainly wasn't period blood. After seeing it, I felt really sick and dirty.

And the smell: I just couldn't get the stench off me. The more I tried to pull away from it, the more it clung to me. It was in my nostrils, it was in my hair. I was becoming nauseous and I retched. It was a certain smell that I just couldn't get away from, a sort of musty dog smell that reminded me vividly of what had happened to me.

At that moment I wasn't able to take in what had occurred. I was confused and wanted to ask somebody, 'What happens if he comes and kills me? My bedroom is downstairs and he could come and break the window or whatever, and what happens if nobody believes me?' I had these mad thoughts of self-hatred, self-blame and self-harm. With Huntley, I had been so near to death, which is why now I consider life to be priceless.

I wasn't aware of the long-term significance of what Huntley had just done to me. I wasn't aware that it was an abhorrent sex act. I wasn't able to fully comprehend what he had done in terms of right and wrong. What didn't pass through my mind was that he had no right to have done that. No, I didn't think, He has got no right doing that and I am going to tell my mum and get the police in.

That is not to say that I hadn't been made aware of 'strangers' and so on. I was aware, but I just thought these warnings related to strange men, not those you knew already. I mean, Huntley was considered a family friend. I didn't even know what there was to fear about strangers, other than that they could take me away. No one had said, 'Don't let strange men fiddle with you down there, or even men you know.'

There was a man down the street one time who waved me over – I was only about seven – and asked, 'Are you Mandy's daughter?'

'Yes, yes,' I replied.

And then he moved a bit closer and said he was something to do with Auntie Bet. She was related to my granddad, but I'm not sure how; all I can remember is she had loads and loads of cats.

This man was her friend and I just said, 'Oh, right.'

He was putting boxes into the boot of his car and he asked, 'How's your mum?

'She's fine, thank you,' I answered.

As he handed me 50 pence he chirped, 'Here you are, duck.'

I can remember going in and joyfully telling my mum as I held out my hand to show her this nice shiny coin, 'Look, Mum, I just got 50 pence off that man down the road.'

Mum froze and sternly demanded, 'What man?'

Innocently I replied, 'The man who is putting boxes into the back of his car. He knows you.'

'What bloody man?' Mum snapped as she stood up, went and opened the door and craned her neck out to see the man for herself. With relief in her voice, she said it was this man called Rob. But she warned me, 'Mind, don't you ever go near anybody whether they say, "Oh, I know your mum" or "I know your dad" or whatever.'

I tried to explain to Mum that it was only because he said, 'I know Mandy, you know. Mandy, your mum...'

Mum stopped me short when she hammered her point home: 'Don't go near anybody who says that or anybody who says, "Come with me", OK?'

'No, Mum,' I said respectfully. 'I'll never do it again.'

So I knew at that age not to talk to or accept money from strangers, but to me Huntley wasn't a stranger. So back then I was double wary of strangers and, as I said, Huntley wasn't one, just as he wasn't to Holly and Jessica.

He had built up trust within the community and held a responsible job, so who would think a school caretaker could take the lives of two children when he had been passed fit to be around them?

In total, Huntley came to the attention of the Humberside Police on ten occasions. In addition, between August 1995 and July 1998, he was reported to North East Lincolnshire Social Services on five separate occasions. Unbelievably, three of the reports alleging underage sex were passed on, independently of each other, to the Humberside Police.

I lay the blame squarely at the doors of North East Lincolnshire Social Services and the Humberside Police. From the Introduction to this book and what I say later, you will see why.

After kicking my clothes into the corner of the bathroom, I ran the water from just the hot tap: it was the hottest bath I've ever had. My feet and hands were really cold and I had a sick and ill feeling within me as I got into the bath. As I sat in that hot water I just wanted to dissolve into it and let it consume me, let it cleanse me through and through.

But the water on its own wasn't removing the remnants of Huntley from me. I felt repulsed at what he had done; my body was screaming out to be purified.

I remember seeing the bottle of bleach and then a small brush, like a nailbrush, really thick. I had to get rid of that rancid smell, so I undid the yellow cap on the bottle and slowly poured the bleach over what I saw as Huntley's calling card. I tried to scrub away in a mad frenzy what Huntley had done to me. As I scrubbed, the area became red-raw. My skin was starting to blister.

Although I was cleansing the superficial film of Huntley's filthy touch from the outside of me, my insides were churning and my stomach was in knots. I was at the end of my tether as I reached out and picked up the bottle again. I pushed down the childproof cap and unscrewed it, then immersed the part-filled bottle in the water and let it fill. I wanted to really cleanse the stench of Huntley away. I felt soiled and sick. The hurt of that dirty, shameful nightmare was horrendous.

As my hands clenched in tension around the plastic bottle, part of me had shut down and the only way I could deal with the torment was by gulping down the cocktail of chemical and bathwater. As the hot toxic brew entered my mouth, I prayed that the liquid filling me would wash away my living nightmare. How much of the mix I swallowed, I don't really know. I just kept gulping it down. I didn't care, so long as I could get that monster's stench off me and out of me. If only I could have washed away the pain that easily. The realisation that I was never going to be the same person again was dawning on me.

I thought I must be a dirty, horrible person and I was trying to wash it away. But it wouldn't go away. And, when I couldn't wash it away, I decided to push it deep down within me. I locked it away behind a mask of self-hatred.

Looking back, I don't know how I didn't kill myself by what I did. It wasn't something I had planned; it was just a spontaneous act on seeing the bleach bottle. The contents were stronger than soap and I knew it was used for deep cleaning. I had no intention of killing myself, I just had to get rid of this smell, because what if anyone could smell it on me? What if they found out I had been out of the street with Huntley? Then I'd really be in for it. I needed to wash the stench of Huntley's breath from my mouth, too.

I was ill for the rest of that night. Between my legs it burned from my scrubbing. I got my pyjamas on and sought the soothing comfort of my bed. Mum sensed something was amiss and asked, 'Is everything all right? Did you have a good time?'

Although I longed to confide in her, I just couldn't find the words, so I buried the pain in my reply, 'Yes, thank you. I don't feel very well. I'm off to bed.'

As I walked towards my bedroom, I bit down hard on my lip, praying that I wouldn't burst into an uncontrollable flood of tears in front of Mum. I just couldn't bring myself to tell her what Huntley had done to me. I resigned myself to a life of bitter silence. In time, the pain of silence would become too much to bear.

When I closed the bedroom door, all of the ache inside me welled up and spilled out as tears of pain rolled down my cheeks. I felt so numb, lost and alone.

I was terrified of what might happen to me, as I was in the downstairs bedroom on my own. He only lives a few minutes away, I thought. He could come to my window easily at nine o'clock at night, put it through and kill me, and everyone is upstairs.

That night, as I lay there, it all came hurtling back to haunt me. I can remember literally twiddling my thumbs out of nervousness: 50 times one way and then 50 times the other way. Things started to come to the front of my mind, but I was running on autopilot, twiddling until my thumbs ached.

What am I doing that for? I thought. I kept going over what had happened during the day and thinking, I really, really, really want to tell somebody but what happens if he comes to kill me? Exhausted from the torment, I fell asleep.

A few hours later, about three o'clock, an uncomfortable feeling of dampness awakened me. I had wet the bed. I had never done it before, and I was quite embarrassed for myself. I tried to conceal this from Mum and didn't tell her.

The next day – well, a few hours later – I remember just staying in the sanctuary of the house, but then I started worrying. What if Huntley were to knock on the door and come after me?

The odd thing is that Katie never made any effort to come and see me after that fateful day when Huntley took me to 'climb trees', which was unusual. I, obviously, wasn't going to call on Katie, because Huntley was there.

I don't know the reason for Katie Webber's withdrawal from my life immediately after that sunny Saturday afternoon when Huntley turned his evil thoughts into reality. But it has to be considered very strange that she didn't even come along for the regular Saturday trip into town. The longest length of time she had stayed away before that was about three or four days.

No one even asked why I never went around to Katie's. It was as if she had never existed. At some point, I thought, she would have called to see me to ask why I hadn't been going there. I was quite surprised and thinking, Why hasn't she come along to see me?

She never even came to see what happened on the Saturday she had called for me, the day she had hurriedly left and said she would see me at her place. Surely that warranted some explanation?

As time went on, I was having flashbacks to the sex attack. I was finding it increasingly difficult to contain it within me. I felt it would only take some stupid thing to trigger the release mechanism within me and I would spill the beans on Huntley's crimes.

This is exactly what happened one day in July 1998 when a fête was taking place next to our local church in Humberston. The venue was what is called the Paddock, where the swings are, and they usually had bric-a-brac stalls and other attractions.

My friend knocked on the door and asked, 'Are you coming out to the fête today, Hailey?'

'Yes,' I said enthusiastically.

No sooner had I spoken than my mum came out of nowhere and overruled me: 'No!'

In stark disbelief I pleaded with her, 'Oh, what's the matter, why?'

To my relief, Mum said, 'Not until you've tidied your room.'

'OK,' I groaned, and told my friend, 'I'll meet you there in half an hour.'

'It'll take you longer than half an hour to clean your bedroom,' Mum said.

OK then, I thought. But by this time I had an attitude like: I don't care what anybody says, I will do what I want and nobody has the upper hand with me. I'm a big girl and, if you want to mess with me now, you mess with me.

I cleaned my bedroom quickly by putting everything under my bed and under my quilt, all my mucky clothes and things, and then cheerfully announced, 'I'm finished. I'll walk to the fair now.'

'No, you are not,' Mum insisted.

'Why not?' I moaned.

She barked back, 'Your bedroom is still bloody messy and this is getting ridiculous. Keep your room tidy. It used to be nice and tidy, why isn't it tidy now?'

After the Huntley attack, I must admit, my whole

outlook on life seemed to have changed overnight. The experience had a dramatic effect on my character. Whereas once I would be polite and wore party dresses and had long hair, now I was dressing down, trying to make myself as unattractive as possible. I cut my ponytail, shunned dresses in favour of trousers and became a rebellious teenager.

My bedroom was downstairs, facing the garden. The fête was a tantalising thought. So, when Mum was out of sight, I shut my bedroom door, jumped out of the window and scampered off to the Paddock with an arrogant air about me.

There I met up with all my friends, and after about 15 minutes I spotted the local bobby, PC Andy Woods. It turned out that he had been to our house for a coffee to see how my mum was. My dad was a special constable and Andy, as well as being a policeman, was a friend of the family.

Mum had got nattering with him and she had a strop on about the state of my room and how I had slipped away to the fête. She said to Andy, 'If you see Hailey when you're at the fête, will you pick her up and bring her home, please, because she shouldn't have gone.'

'I'll get in my car and go now,' Andy told her.

And this was why he rolled up at the fête. All the school kids knew Andy because he was an all right copper. A girl called Danielle Hattersley knew that I had absconded out of my bedroom window to come to the fête and she went over and greeted Andy, 'All right, PC Woods, how are things?'

He replied, 'Oh, great. I'm looking for Hailey.'

Innocently or self-importantly, I don't know which, Danielle informed him, 'She's over there in them bushes with all her mates.'

Andy came over to me and said, 'Come on, then, Hailey. I've got to take you home.'

I was mega-embarrassed in front of all my friends, thinking, Mum has got him to do this. I don't believe this, it's a farce. All my mates are here and how embarrassing is that?

After a show of dumb insolence, I got into his little panda car and he drove me home. We'd only just pulled up at the door when all of a sudden my mum began shouting at me. I was at a loss as to why she was going on like this.

PC Woods ordered, 'Go on, Hailey, go and sit down.'

I sat down without a word and she started screaming blue murder. 'You could get kidnapped. I can't believe that you are putting me through this. I have already told you, you are not going out until you have tidied your bedroom.'

All this because I didn't do a good enough job on my room. 'I *have* tidied my bedroom,' I said in mock disbelief.

'Like what, putting all your crap underneath your bed?' she ranted.

I brazened it out, then snapped defensively, 'Well, it's tidier than what it was this morning, so it *is* tidier now,' and lamely finished with a sullen, 'you know'.

'Lose the attitude,' she fumed.

I just sat there and took my telling off with her screeching voice ringing in my ears. As the scolding went on, it filled my head, got louder and built up to a crescendo. She was incandescent as she raged, 'You could get kidnapped. You could get raped one day. You could get murdered.'

I broke my silence angrily. 'I don't care what you've got to say.'

At this, Mum seethed, 'Well, you will care when one day you end up getting really hurt or you end up getting raped.'

By this time, I think I understood what rape was, and maybe that's what Huntley had done to me. I didn't need this ear-bashing. After all, my life had been turned upside down and I only had a thin veneer of tolerance.

As soon as the keywords 'raped' and 'murdered' had been thrown at me, they unlocked the floodgates that had been holding back my secret horror for some ten months, since September 1997. My flashbacks took me into another dimension, one of lurking demons.

I had had this bollocking going on against me for half an hour when I stood up and unleashed my torment. '*I have been raped*,' I screamed.

This brought a sudden end to her tirade and you could hear a pin drop as, her eyes bulging, she gasped, 'Eh!'

'I have been,' I blurted.

'What do you mean?'

'Nothing, nothing.'

I got up to walk out and our policeman friend stood there and brusquely ordered, 'You are not going anywhere. Sit down.'

And by that time, because I'd had to bury the pain deep within me and had lived alone with the agonising torture that was tearing me apart for so long, I exploded with anger, 'Just get out of my way, just leave me alone. He'll kill me!'

As far as I was concerned, I *had* been raped. My interpretation of rape was what had happened to me. As it happens, rape would have been less enduring than a whole afternoon at the hands of Huntley's repeated and unremitting barrage of sexual assaults. Rape would have been over and done with far quicker than the prolonged and agonising torment that I suffered at Huntley's evil, filthy hands. So, as far as I was concerned, yes, I had been raped.

Mum's face was ashen as she searched for a response. 'Talk to me, Hailey. Who by?'

All this ice was running through my body. I knew by that time that Huntley had moved away. I didn't know where to, as he had left a month earlier, but I now felt able to reveal the horrific suffering I had undergone.

Then Mum's face softened as she tentatively asked the heart-wrenching question every mother dreads: 'Do you know what rape means?'

Not knowing anything other than *my* definition of the word, I said, 'Yes.'

As she held back her tears, Mum apologised, 'Right, sorry. Who by?'

Overcome with the fear of God, I edged my way closer to revealing the name of my secret tormentor, and then I quickly blurted, 'By that Ian down the road.'

Mum's demeanour had changed to that of a woman at war, and as the fire came into her eyes she stormed, 'Ian who?'

I held back the tears of pain as I stuttered, 'Katie Webber's boyfriend.'

The fury in my mum's voice cut through me when she spat out, 'What's his last name?'

'Huntley or Hunter,' I said timidly.

This news was like a bolt of lightning and she was aghast.

PC Woods was lost for words as he stumbled out. 'I'm going to call in the special police, the people who deal with this kind of thing, the sexual side of things.'

On hearing that, Mum demanded, 'I want a special trained police officer that can deal with this.'

She then gathered herself and said in a soothing tone, 'Do you want me to wait here and comfort you when they call or do you want me to stand in the kitchen out of the way to save your embarrassment?'

Embarrassed at what Mum would overhear, I told her, 'Will you go in the kitchen, please.'

It will be fine, I thought, if it's just me and this police officer that calls; it's not going to go any further.

Later, when the police officer arrived, my heart raced in turmoil as I saw that it was a man, not the woman officer I had been expecting! Mum wasn't very happy, either, because she knew that I would be shy, that I would hold back with a man.

So the ginger-haired policeman came in, but I did not feel reassured or calmed as he started, 'Right then, what's your name?'

This male police officer took the details from me and wrote them down. His tone appeared to me to be disconcerting and gruff. 'What's your name?'

'Hailey,' I tentatively replied.

'Right, Hailey. How old are you?'

'Twelve.'

'What has happened then?'

I was practically lost for words. Here was a male police officer seeking answers to questions from a minor, a female, about a sex attack. I was lured, groomed and abused. I couldn't just tell this man all of that. I didn't know where to start because I was really embarrassed. What do I say? I thought. I can't tell him all that happened.

I remember going through the details and I mentioned with embarrassment about being fingered and he leaned right forward and demanded, 'Do you know what being fingered means?'

As his question hit me with the grace of an elephant landing on jelly, I wanted the ground to open up and swallow me whole. I couldn't get involved in this process because I felt really embarrassed. I didn't want to say yes, but in my head I was thinking, Well, of course I know what it means if I've had it done to me.

I was pleased to see the back of the policeman when he left, as I just didn't feel comfortable spilling my guts out to a man, not initially, as a female child victim.

The police said to my mum that they would be in touch with her and would stay in touch. After a wait of about three or four weeks, they came back and told her that Huntley had denied it. Well, what did they think he would do? Give a signed confession with a photo? Huntley knew the heat was on. He would now lie through his teeth just to get out of it whenever he could. The proof of this is what happened in Soham in 2002, when he got his partner Maxine Carr to lie for him to the police about his whereabouts right after Holly and Jessica disappeared.

Later on, though, from behind the bars of prison, Huntley would lay the blame at Carr's door when he accused her of having told him what to say and do to escape conviction for the Soham murders. Here was further proof of how far Huntley would go to exert control over others, even after he was jailed.

In my case, eventually the police arrested Huntley in Cleethorpes and, after questioning, he was subsequently released without charge.

After Huntley was convicted, he admitted to his parents on a prison visit that he had lied under oath about the circumstances of one of the murders, Jessica's. I wonder what else Huntley is holding back?

A lone female police officer came to see Mum and me to tell us that nothing was being done, basically, because there wasn't enough evidence.

They had taken statements from my brother Hayden, James Webber, Huntley and me, and I was led to believe that Huntley's father had given him an alibi by saying that he was with him on the day of my allegation. An alibi given some ten months after the crime was relied upon. I look back on it and I think the tail was wagging the dog.

From the evidence to hand at the time of writing, we can see that he was certainly known to the police for allegations of a sexual nature against him. Under caution, he even admitted to a police constable that he had had sex with a girl of 15.

And that was that. The short inquiry was finished.

But what they did have was a catalogue of allegations: rape, a discontinued rape case, statements from various people. The same can be said of social services: they were aware of the allegations against Huntley and, as a direct result of their failings and even, in some cases, their dereliction of duty, I suffered.

Unbelievably, the chief executive of North East Lincolnshire Council, Jim Leivers, defended social workers' handling of Huntley when he said, 'The five cases were from different areas, involved different circumstances and were handled by different people, who had no reason to cross refer with one another.'

And he went on to say, 'None of the girls would make a complaint about Huntley, to whom they referred as their "boyfriend". We are not here to arrest offenders; we are interested in protecting youngsters. We were confident these were good parents and we saw no reason to continue involvement. This is a character that, as soon anybody gets a sniff, he was off. He was particularly keen not to get involved with any agencies like social services and police.'

Well, I can tell you, Huntley did have contact with social services, as he phoned them. Social services actually mishandled a number of cases – mine was one of them – and, as a consequence, they were slammed in a report.

I also blame the former Chief Constable of the Humberside Police, David Westwood, for allowing my allegation that Huntley had assaulted me to be wiped from his force's records after the police had interviewed Huntley but taken no action.

Not long after, at the time the police told us about the case being dropped, Huntley appeared in a newspaper. My mum kept a clipping and she showed me it not long after, when she revealed, 'You're not the only person he has done it to. Look in the paper.'

It read: 'Ian Kevin Huntley arrested for attempted rape', or something like that. This was a gas-alley rape and then the case was dropped and my mum said, 'Don't worry, duck, he'll get caught one day.'

I felt that my whole world had fallen to pieces. Why doesn't anybody believe me, I thought, and why is nobody saying we are going to have him or anything like that? After the police said the case file was passed to the CPS, we found out it was never passed to them. I learned that only recently. They told me that it was never passed to the CPS; it never got through the main doors of the CPS, it was passed to PS Tait, who concluded that there was insufficient evidence for there to be a realistic prospect of conviction.'

Utter bollocks is what I say to that. Although Sir Christopher Kelly slammed the police and social services in a report, I have only just started slamming them myself.

In my view, the law should allow for a man like Huntley to be prosecuted by virtue of having a string of sexual allegations against him and claims of dalliances with underage girls. In the event, he was not prosecuted.

Huntley, an asthma sufferer, bullied and nicknamed 'Spadehead' on account of his large forehead, had, as I mentioned earlier, previously admitted to a policeman that he had sexual intercourse with a 15-year-old girl and signed the interview sheet to this effect. Yet he escaped being charged or even having a caution lodged against him because the girl failed to complain. This, the police say, is their reason for not prosecuting Huntley over that little matter of unlawful sexual intercourse! That should have had some influence on the decision makers supposedly concerned with the allegations I made against Huntley.

Naturally, I was not surprised when I learned that his first girlfriend, Amanda Marshall, by the time she was 16, had moved in with the 17-year-old Huntley. Their relationship had started going down the slippery slope when Amanda discovered he had started bringing other girls back to their flat when she was out.

Soon after this, Huntley overdosed and Amanda returned, locked in a dependency on him for her self-esteem and, in turn, his need to control her grew.

Would you be surprised to learn that Amanda, in a bid to make the relationship work, accompanied Huntley to sessions with a psychiatrist! Already, in 1994, the signs were there when she became pregnant with his child but miscarried after he threw her down the stairs. This is the same year that Huntley's mother left his father for her lesbian lover, Julie Beasley.

In December 1994, Huntley met 18-year-old Claire
Evans, an RAF administrator, and after a short affair
they married in January 1995. The marriage was
doomed to failure when the 21-year-old Huntley
claimed his 18-year-old brother Wayne slept with
Claire on their wedding night. In a wedding ceremony
in 2000, Claire married Wayne.

At the Bichard Inquiry, Detective Chief
Superintendent Gavin Baggs acknowledged failure
after failure regarding lack of training within the
intelligence-saving system of Humberside Police.
Under cross-examination by the Inquiry his exact
words were: '...there was this general misunderstanding
which I accept was regrettable ... and I do accept that
that is a failure.'

Unbelievably, no records of the previous allegations
against Huntley 1, 2, 3, 4 and 9 [these numbers refer to
the system of numbering incidents in the Inquiry]
managed to make it to the police's CIS Nominals
system. There was also an acceptance among police staff
that they hadn't been adequately trained and it was
accepted that officers were disgruntled at being
'overworked and understaffed', as DCS Gavin Baggs
conceded at the Bichard Inquiry.

In what I consider one of the more generously
proportioned blunders of the Humberside Police that
was not unearthed until the Humberside Police carried
out an investigation for the purpose of their

submissions to the Bichard Inquiry, DCS Baggs admitted that the Humberside Force knew that Huntley was using the name Nixon, but that information did not get transposed from his manual record on to the CIS Nominals.

In response to being asked, 'That in your view, I take it, was a pretty serious failing?' DCS Baggs replied, 'It was in retrospect a serious failing, yes. It is a failing that had very severe knock-on consequences, yes.'

Unbelievable. A total cock-up was responsible for the fact that Huntley was not correctly vetted for his caretaker's job.

It was alleged that in August 1995 Huntley had a 13-year-old boy and the boy's 15-year-old sister living with him in Grimsby. The girl's father claimed to the police that Huntley had been having unlawful sexual intercourse with the girl, which she appears to have informally confirmed. This resulted in Huntley admitting everything to PC Teasdale under caution when interviewed at his home. Huntley signed the interview statement, and his exact words were: 'If her parents were OK about it, it was not an offence.' Why wasn't Huntley charged?

Which leads me back to the Bichard Inquiry and the questioning of DCS Baggs on 3 March 2004 over this matter.

This is what DCS Baggs said about why Huntley was not charged or even cautioned over the matter of unlawful sexual intercourse with a minor in August 1995: 'The test that is applied in terms of whether or not someone should be cautioned for any offence is initially the sufficiency of evidence test, as has been alluded to. The sufficiency of evidence test is based on whether or not there is sufficient evidence for there to be a likelihood of a successful prosecution. In considering this particular crime, at the time that Mr Billam made his decision, it is my view – and of course this might not be the same view as everyone else – but it is my view that there was not sufficient evidence to make it likely that there could be a successful prosecution because there was no signed statement from the victim in this case. The evidence in the Officer's notebook was hearsay evidence and could not have been introduced into a court case, as I understand it, so we are left with a situation where the only evidence that is in a suitable format for introduction in a potential court case is the confession evidence in the interview record which Huntley had himself signed. So it is my opinion – and I have in the past been the head of the Admin and Justice Unit where these policies are set – it is my opinion that there was insufficient evidence as it stood at that time to properly authorise a caution.'

To the credit of the Bichard team, I should add that one of them said to DCS Baggs, 'I am grateful for that. You are aware, of course, that others within the force and HMIC take a potentially different view in relation to incident 1 and the appropriateness or otherwise of issuing a caution?'

DCS Baggs answered, 'I am aware of that. Certainly within the force, at the time of the chronology document being put together, there were divided opinions. I think that, within the force now, those divided opinions are much more reconciled along the view that I have just expressed. I am aware that the HMIC also takes a different view. Perhaps I could just take it one stage further. Although at the moment, at the time when Mr Billam made his decision, it is certainly my opinion that there was insufficient evidence to justify an appropriate caution, it is possible – and we will never know now, I expect – but it is possible that by doing some further work we could have reached a situation where a caution could have been justified because, although the complainant in that case had expressed a view that there should be no action taken against her boyfriend, it does appear to me, at least, that she was not being obstructive insofar as she has actually given a verbal account and signed the pocket book. Whether she would have been prepared to go that one stage further and sign the written statement, I do not know, but it is possible that with some more work we could have reached that situation where a caution would have been appropriate.'

Had Huntley received a police caution, he would have been more detectable in future searches on the police's criminal intelligence database. Personally, I am less than happy at what I have learned about police incompetence in this matter.

In response to DCS Baggs's answer just quoted, a further question was put to him at the Bichard Inquiry: 'In your view, with the benefit of hindsight, is that work that you think should desirably have been taken?'

DCS Baggs replied, 'I do not know exactly what Mr Billam was presented with and he made a decision on all of the facts before him at the time, and maybe he had information before him that I am not in possession of.'

A follow-up question was put to DCS Baggs: 'Thank you. Let us go to contact three, the incident number 3, which is the second of the unlawful sexual intercourse allegations that appears to have come to the attention of the police on 22 May 1996. Again, I want to concentrate on the record-keeping and creation so far as this is concerned. You have already expressed the view that it would have been desirable and helpful to have created a record on CIS Nominals in relation to incident 1. Does it follow that the substance of your answer is the same in relation to this incident, namely that although you say in 12.1: "With the information obtained from the original police officers … [Reading to the words] … in relation to this contract", and so on, your view is that a record should have been made on

CIS Nominals in relation to this incident also? Paragraph 12, 0070 0086.'

DCS Baggs: 'I am just trying to remind myself of the full details of contact. It is contact three we are referring to, is it not?'

Follow-up question to DCS Baggs: 'It is. You will see in 12.1 how you deal with it. You do not express a view one way or the other. In relation to the earlier incident you had said you would not have expected it and it was not normal practice but that matter does not...'

DCS Baggs: 'No, I remained silent on this one.'

Follow-up question to DCS Baggs: 'Sorry, at 14.1 you say "would not be expected". If you want to have a look at that as well, 14.1?'

DCS Baggs: 'Yes. I say it will not be expected in this case because we did not actually get involved in the investigation at all and the decision was made by Mr Billam again to leave this matter with the Social Services, so on that basis I would not expect anyone within my organisation to submit that intelligence for entry on our criminal-intelligence system.'

Follow-up question to DCS Baggs: 'The fact of the allegation though, in retrospect, surely, would have been information which it was important to recall? It was information about an allegation of the sort of offence in relation to which he had already made a confession nine months earlier. He had been given the sternest warning. Even though he had not been formally cautioned, he knew the form in relation to having sex with underage girls and here he was alleged to have done it again.'

DCS Baggs: 'Yes.'

Follow-up question to DCS Baggs: 'It would surely have been helpful to have had some record, if only of the allegation, and with whatever specific reliability grade you chose to put on it, but some record surely would have been helpful in relation to incident 3?'

DCS Baggs: 'Again, clearly with the benefit of hindsight then some record would have been very helpful, but at the time – and in this document I have tried to comment on what people did at the time and whether it was appropriate or not – and at that time, of course, as far as we could tell, there was no recognition of a previous incident because there was no URN, no record from the previous contact created.'

Follow-up question to DCS Baggs: 'But it was no record, was it not? You started saying "No URN", and corrected yourself rightly, because there was no record on CIS Nominals?'

DCS Baggs: 'That is quite right, yes.'

When I look at all these failings and how Huntley was able to get a job working in a Cambridgeshire school with children after having been investigated over my allegation and further allegations, I am filled with disbelief. From the onset of the Soham investigation, it

Growing up …

Above left: Two years old and blissfully unaware of what life had in store for me.

Above right: The child anyone would wish for – five years old and not a care in the world.

Below left: A happy bridesmaid, aged nine.

Below right: At eleven years old, approximately one month before the attack.

Above: This picture still fills me with fear – the orchard where Huntley attacked me.

Below: The pub that was situated near the place of my attack.

The pictures on this page and the pages that follow show me being interviewed by the police about the attack. I think my body language clearly shows how very difficult it was for me to talk about what had happened.

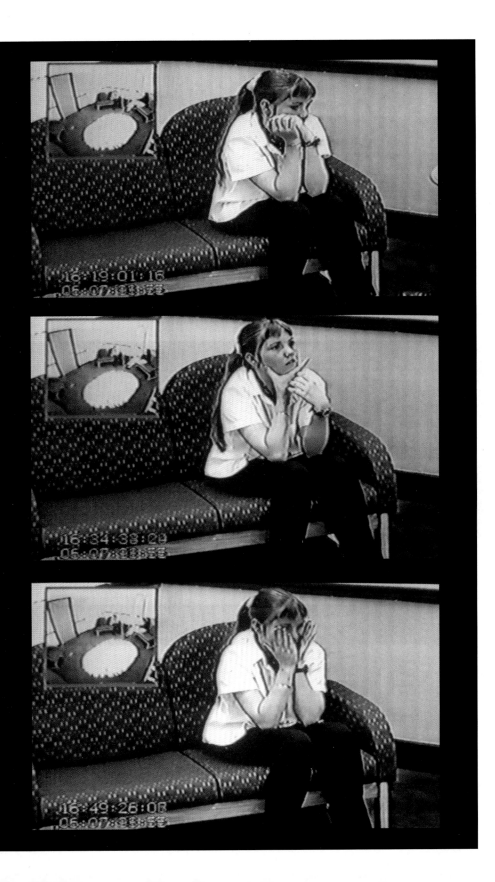

Above left: My Grandad, who I adored and who was my best friend and, *inset*, the Pea Bung, my favourite place to go for fish and chips when I was younger.

Above right: The nightmares begin.

Below: With Colin in 2003.

The happiest day of my life.

Despite the trauma of my past, I am determined to develop a career in modelling.

took the police nearly two weeks to become aware of the previous sexual allegations against Ian Huntley. Also, early on during the investigation, his story was not even checked out as regards his whereabouts.

But this can lead on to things such as when I made the complaint to the police. I have said to this day that it was always questioned that when it came out they said they were going to get a special unit in from the police department, a lady that would come and chat with me. After all this, I thought, Thank God I am speaking to a woman or girl or whatever, and then this man rolled up and he just sat there with his notebook.

In 2004, when the investigation into my allegation was brought to light again, in tears I said to the lady, 'What happens if I'm not believed?'

She asked, 'Why?'

'Because,' I said, 'I can't remember whether I told this copper that was interviewing me or taking notes, whether he [Huntley] had inserted his fingers into me or not, because I can remember feeling embarrassed with him being a man.'

After the attack was reported to the police, to some of my family members I was the biggest whore walking. But, if that was the case, I was a dead whore walking. My soul had become pickled and lost. I endured quite a bit of spitefulness, and I don't know why. This isn't just about Huntley, it is about the whole lot of them. All are as bad as each other. I was goaded by my brothers and even branded a cow and similar names. I saw myself as worthless and saw no way out of the mess in which I had become embedded.

Really, though, there was only one person that was able to lift me from my quagmire of misery. Nobody could make me feel the love of mankind as much as my granddad could. Forget therapists and child psychologists. What happened to the old shoulder to cry on? People have grown apart and modern living has killed off the old-style doorstep counselling.

Thinking back to when I was about 14, I don't know if Granddad knew about Huntley's attack on me. Maybe Mum told him in confidence and, if she did, he never let on. I feel, in retrospect, that he could have changed something but then sometimes I'm glad that he didn't know because it would have broken his heart knowing that somebody had done that to me.

Anyway, returning to how things have gone wrong in terms of law and order: murders, stabbings, shootings, drinking, drugging, raping, mugging. Ideally, you are brought up to learn how to respect people and their possessions and to respect and look after your own. People who are doing those bad things have not learned respect for others or themselves. They have not been mentored or shown the right way. I know that if I kicked someone's car window in I would get a fine. But these people aren't getting the right message.

By this, I mean the justice system in this country

stinks. I think they would rather punish the innocent and let the guilty just go away and carry on. I am able to say that after what has happened to me, and my experience has brought the issue to the fore for me. More understanding is given to the criminal than the victim.

Criminals should be made to pay for their crimes and made to show respect to their victim. But instead, the way the justice system works now, I think the people whose job it is to punish crime are too worried about people like Ian Huntley; they are too worried about his rights and his needs. The European Court protects that bastard's rights. Who protects mine?

He has committed a crime and he is in prison, where nobody from outside can get to him. Now if somebody from outside wanted to stab him, they wouldn't get the chance because they can't get close enough to him. Others behind bars can get him, but with every attack that is made on him – whether it's hot water thrown over him or whatever – he will sue the Prison Service and come up smelling of roses as well as receiving a big payout.

But what's to stop that sort of attack from happening to me? Who is there to protect me if anything like that happens? I know things will happen to Huntley in prison, but I would not like to see him murdered, as that is too good for him. Leave him to suffer behind bars as I am suffering, in a prison of his making. Let us see who lasts the longest. Maybe I could sue him for the money he will win from being attacked. There's poetic justice for you.

Huntley and other supermonsters, like Ian Brady, make me feel sick. These criminals are mentally flawed by a weakness that controls them and they will never be cured, no matter how much therapy, medication or shock treatment they get. I have looked into the eyes of Huntley and survived. I know what makes him tick.

I can also say that, if Huntley had been prosecuted over one of the sexual allegations but not sent to prison, or if he had just been put on file or on the Sex Offenders' Register, he would never have got that job in that school, as he would have been more closely monitored and probably would not have had that opportunity to kill. Even so, I do believe that, given the chance, Huntley would have killed or tried to kill in order to silence his victim – it was only a matter of when – but it may not have been a double killing.

In a nutshell, Huntley was born evil. Obviously, that's easy for me to say, but I do think about society and, if he had been punished for a crime that he did to me nine years ago, would he have gone on to murder Jessica Chapman and Holly Wells in 2002? There are people who are inherently evil and no amount of badgering and cajoling, or respect or education, by society does any good when they are determined to commit evil acts.

My task now is to prevent Huntley from ever being

unleashed on society again. If ever he is released, he will still be an evil person; he will still have the same evil within him in 40 years' time as he had when he assaulted me. His evilness was there from day one. His soul and his whole character are evil. But I do believe that his childhood played a major part in what he has become. I think that when he was a child he was never given any control, no say in what happened in his life. That is why I think he is now such a control freak, crazed by power.

In his mind he made me into his possession. He wanted to control me, like the others in his life, like turning a tap on and off. But, in the end, he just couldn't stop his own dark heart doing what it wanted and going even further in this quest for power over others.

In addition to my aim to see this murderer stay locked up, I'm still determined that lessons should be learned by those who made massive blunders in the Huntley case. What really angers me is that the police logged the allegation I made against Huntley as 'stranger abuse'. I only found this out near the end of 2005. Can you imagine how I feel now at the failings of those in power? This terminology, 'stranger abuse', even if in police terms technically accurate to distinguish from an attack by a family member, for example, seemed to me to be completely misplaced in my case. Huntley was known to me, known for some time. The damning North East Lincolnshire Area Child

Protection Committee Report into Ian Huntley (for the period 1995 to 2001), headed by Sir Christopher Kelly, suggests that I might have been at further risk of harm from Huntley. Too right. For years I lived in fear that he would come crashing through my window and murder me. Even now, I awake with a start at the slightest unfamiliar noise.

The 2004 report also noted 'the apparently very hands-off approach taken by social services to what was obviously a very troubled time for MN [me] after the assault'.

Earlier that year the Bichard Inquiry, conducted by Sir Michael Bichard, was also highly critical of the investigation into Huntley's previous allegations and suggested that the intelligence system of the Humberside Police, which dealt with some of the cases, was 'fundamentally flawed' and that the force's child-protection database was 'largely worthless'.

The then Chief Constable of the Humberside Police, David Westwood, has much to answer for in the systems failure, which allegedly 'failed to identify Ian Huntley as a danger'.

I just wish those that I told about Huntley had said that they believed me and taken a more proactive approach. I can't get rid of this bitterness within me. Why am I left feeling that my allegation could have been dealt with more thoroughly and sensitively? I wish with all my heart that the police had prosecuted on the basis of my complaint and those of the other girls allegedly assaulted by Ian Huntley.

What also infuriates me is how, in one of the reports after Soham, the 15-year-old-girls Huntley had sex with were referred to as 'young women', as if, somehow, their maturity being exaggerated in this way would make them look less vulnerable and so make the offence seem less than it was. In the eyes of the law they were minors: *girls, not* young women.

Huntley's pattern of behaviour deviated from his predatory, exploitative relationships with girls in their mid-teens when he carried out that brutal sex attack against me. I was supposedly the first much younger girl that he sexually assaulted. But had he carried out this sort of attack on other girls of my age and younger before he did what he did to me?

The dark cloud of paedophilia that has stalked the Soham case has revealed how easy it was for Huntley to work with children. While the police and the government were at war over who was to blame for the shocking situation in which information about Huntley's history of sex allegations was not included in any of his police files, parents mourned the loss of their loved ones.

When I learned of another gigantic blunder made by the Humberside Police – PC Michel Harding recorded allegations that Huntley was a serial sex attacker and on the basis of these allegations added that he was 'likely to continue his activities'; this was put on the force's computer in 1999 by a police officer and wiped off in 2000 – I thought, Clever or what? What a bunch of incompetents!

A leaked report prepared by Her Majesty's Inspectorate of Constabulary revealed a catalogue of incompetence surrounding the Police National Computer. It was taking many forces almost two months to enter details of convictions and arrests on the system: something that should have taken just a week.

This damning document also underlined the ease with which another Huntley could slip through the net! It said, 'There is the potential for known offenders or those suspected of serious offending to be overlooked during the Criminal Review Bureau checks.' This situation left the way open for newly convicted paedophiles to apply for jobs knowing that they were safe from being discovered and so put them in a position to strike undetected, although this flawed system was due to change in 2005. To date, I am unsure whether it has changed or not.

Apart from locking him up, of course, what Huntley's conviction has done is to open a can of worms. It has revealed a grim picture of confusion created by the Data Protection Act and exacerbated by the Human Rights Act over what information police can keep about suspected paedophiles.

In my opinion, blame was fairly apportioned to the

two Chief Constables at the centre of the Huntley case: Tom Lloyd of Cambridgeshire and David Westwood of Humberside. After all, it was 'check system' mistakes made by the Cambridgeshire Force that resulted in Huntley getting a job at Soham Village College. During police background checks into Huntley on a national police database, his name and date of birth were entered incorrectly. And, like others, I blame many of the investigative problems on David Westwood, formerly Chief Constable of Humberside, who failed to identify Huntley as a danger, even though I had said in a police video interview in 1998, when I was 12, that Huntley had sexually assaulted me. I hope this extract from that interview will convince you of my sincerity about my allegation:

Police officer: Can you tell me, what do you think made Huntley allow you to leave the woods?

Hailey: Because I told him that my mum worked at the Grosvenor and that I had agreed to meet her there.

Police officer: So what did he say when you left him in the woods?

Hailey: He said if I told anyone what had happened or wrote anything in a diary that he would come and kill me and I then ran away from him and he chased me.

Police officer: Had you had any problems with

him in the past, I mean did he ever hurt you before?

Hailey: No, never, he was always kind to me.

Police officer: How did you feel when all this was happening to you, Hailey?

Hailey: I kept on saying to myself, 'Oh, why, oh why is this happening to me,' and hoped someone would come and help me, but nobody came.

Police officer: You tell me, Hailey, that you told your brother Hayden about what happened to you three weeks after; what was his reply?

Hailey: He said, 'Oh, you do make up such big lies,' and I said, 'No, honestly. It did really happen.'

Police officer: How do you feel about Ian now?

Hailey: I don't like him very much at all and he makes me feel sick.

Police officer: What do you think should happen to Ian now?

Hailey: I would like to see him prosecuted, for him to understand what he has done to me and to stop him from doing it to anyone else.

Police officer: So you were good friends with Katie Webber, you say. Are you still close now?

Hailey: No, I don't see her now because she stopped seeing me after he did that to me.

Police officer: So you mean, after Ian did that to you, Katie stopped coming to see you, right, after what he did?

Hailey: Yep.

What I can't understand is how easily heads could roll because the government didn't want egg on their face, while I can be walked all over by everyone that has failed me without any recourse.

David Westwood claimed his force had been obliged to 'weed out' accusations against Huntley which did not lead to convictions. The office of the Information Commissioner, the government's data protection watchdog, condemned this claim and for this reason I feel I have recourse against the Humberside Police Force.

Assistant Commissioner David Smith said, 'Their explanation appears to be nonsense from what we know of the information they were keeping.

'The information was clearly relevant to protecting the public and there's nothing in the Data Protection Act or in any guidance we've issued that required them to delete information of such obvious value.'

That is where I rest my case. The police knew of allegations against Huntley and they decided he wasn't even worthy of a few minutes' time and effort to keep his details logged, but they could apply the time and effort, they admit, to 'weed out' his details. This, I say, is an excuse. It would not have been all weeded out back in July 1998, when I made my allegation. Why didn't they act then?

Another thing strikes me as bizarre. The police claim to be deluged with complex guidance on data protection, which they have to pass to their own lawyers, and the police must comply with the legal minefield of the Human Rights Act.

The Humberside Police claimed that, in a case of alleged underage sexual intercourse, they did not prosecute unless a complainant brought a charge. This is rubbish. They prosecuted my prospective husband over that very charge, and named me as the victim. Yet I never raised a complaint – it was my parents that did. The very same police force that failed me has made my life a hell.

To end this chapter, I leave the final words to the Bichard Inquiry, which determined that the Humberside Police Force prepared a file on my case in which there was a confidential disclosure form that was 'inaccurate in almost every respect.'

7

CANNABIS AND WHITE POWDER

MY INNOCENCE NOW STOLEN, THE SUNNY OUTLOOK I ONCE HAD ON LIFE WAS TRANSFORMED AFTER THE ATTACK. My hair still flowed right down to my lower back, and people used to comment, 'Isn't your hair lovely?' or 'I'd love hair like yours.' This was after the attack but before I had revealed to my mum what had happened to me. I used to shy away from them and say, 'Don't touch my hair.' I hated being pawed and gawped at.

I remember one time Mum said she wanted to know about something and, looking back now, it was quite petty and I kicked up a real fuss. I found it hard to deal with stupid little things. If my mum were to say to me, 'You're not going out to the swimming disco on

Thursday if you don't tidy your room,' come Thursday, I wouldn't have done what she had asked me to do.

I stayed in my bedroom all Thursday night and, in a fit of rage, I got some scissors and sheared off all my locks of flaxen hair so it barely reached down to my jaw line.

In those days I just couldn't bear anything. If somebody said no when I expected a yes, or if someone called me a name, I just couldn't handle things like that and it used to really weigh me down.

Sometimes in arguments I would say to my mum, 'I hate you!' She would say, 'I don't like you either.' I would feel like killing myself. Nobody likes me, I used to think. That would be just because one person said they didn't like me. Because of that, I would think that that was what everybody must think.

But getting back to this particular time when I cut all my hair off because I had a disagreement with my mum. The next morning, I woke up and went to the bathroom to do my hair. I could only just fit what was left of my hair into a tiny bobble and then I went downstairs.

Mum was gobsmacked. 'What the hell have you done to your hair?' she burst out.

I reacted furiously: 'Get out of my way. I don't care about you, just leave me alone. I don't want it long.'

Then I went off to school with my hair looking terrible. It was a real messy cut, of course, because I'd just gathered my hair into a bobble and cut it all off.

After that, I started cutting my arms with anything. If I had a bad day at school, I would cut my arms. Because I had control over that, I could stop and start whenever I felt like it. But there was another thing where I had no control: after the attack when I was 11, I used to wet the bed every single night until I was about 14. My planets had collided all right.

When I was cutting my arms, I was being hurt in a controlled way rather than hurt in an uncontrolled way. I could control and tolerate the hurt.

When I was doing this, people didn't notice what was happening, as I was good at concealing it. My main areas of attack were the tops of my arms. I was doing my best to conceal a symptom of what the Huntley attack had done to me. That symptom was the desire not only to blame myself but to physically harm myself.

Several studies of self-harm confirm that it's a serious issue, so I'll give you the details. Studies like Gratz et al. (2002), Van der Kolk, Perry and Herman (1991), and Zlotnick et al. (1996) found that individuals who engage in self-harm report unusually high rates of histories of childhood sexual abuse, childhood physical abuse, emotional neglect, insecure attachment and prolonged separation from caregivers. The first of these in particular applies to my circumstances.

I know self-harm was an abysmal way for a girl of that age to handle the emotional pain, but what else could I do apart from kill myself. In my opinion, I was now worthless and no one liked me. Also, I didn't have the supportive family that any child of that age will benefit from.

Psychologically, I was a wreck and, had I not cracked and revealed what had happened to me, I'm sure I would have killed myself just to escape the ordeal. My self-destruct button had been pressed and I was on a collision course with death.

When I did tell my mum and the police were called in, it was like having a massive weight lifted from my shoulders. I was sure Huntley would be sent to prison for the rest of his life and that would mean he wouldn't be able to come and kill me or anything like that. But, as you now know, the police decided not to do anything and it was all made ten times worse for me because of that. The spectre of Huntley haunts me to this very day, and it will until I get closure on it.

In retrospect, had the police pursued my case to the nth degree, perhaps even got Huntley to court, my belief would in part still be there – although that is easy to say, because he could have appeared in court and been found not guilty. And then would I be saying these things now about how happy I would have been to get him to court? I know that, when I get him into court for this – which I will – that I will win. I have no doubt of that.

The way I look at it now, I see the police begging victims of crime to come forward, and especially in cases like this, as soon as possible after the crime has been committed. It is all very well the men in grey suits saying that, but, in the aftermath of such an intimate violation you can feel somehow as if it is you who is the criminal.

I know I would be able to defend myself against an attack now, but at that time I was only 11. Then again, I think what more than anything else may have saved me from being killed by Huntley was my passiveness.

To me, justice has not been served, even though he is behind bars. Justice has not been delivered. There has been no closure on that score. For me, it still lives on. If Huntley and others can get away with a crime as serious as what he did to me, what other crimes have such criminals got away with? Why has it had to come to murder before it is taken seriously?

My self-image and self-esteem were low, I think, from when the attack happened to me until I started puberty at about 14. I used to dress like a boy. I used to wear boxer shorts to school and my brother's trousers or his school shirts.

Cleanliness was not a strong point as I was still wetting the bed but didn't like taking a bath. I began to have a phobia about getting into the bath because it reminded me of the night I came home and bleached myself from head to toe.

Looking back, I didn't want to make myself look nice or for anybody to compliment me on my hair, my looks or my clothes, or to say, 'God, you are beautiful.' I didn't want any attention whatsoever from men. I wanted to be repulsive; that was my defence. And then nobody would come near me again.

But even though I didn't want praise, when people put me down that also hurt. By making myself repulsive, I was my own worst enemy. It was as though I was trapped and there was no way out. I was caught in a vicious circle: I was never going to get a compliment and therefore I could remain for ever in that little prison I had created for myself, looking unattractive.

At the same time, I longed to be beautiful and to have my long hair and wear make-up and have long nails. But I was still scared that someone would do to me again what Huntley had done. If I kept myself ugly and showed my nastiness at school, maybe it would provoke people into calling me names, and that was what I wanted. This, of course, perpetuated the trap I was in.

In time, I started to get used to the persistent name-calling; it was like water off a duck's back, and I needed a bigger kick. I had progressed to stealing and smoking cannabis, and then there was the white powder, although, when I was admitted for a drugs overdose, the hospital couldn't tell what it was. I was mixing in the wrong circles, but the right circles for my condition.

I didn't know how to cope with the feelings of abandonment, of desolation, that were so strong within me. I didn't know what was happening to me, but I now know that it was post-traumatic stress disorder, but who cared?

My relationship with my family had sunk to an all-time low. I had gone off the rails and my eldest brothers, Ben, Adam and Hayden, used to call me names. To them, I was a druggy, a thief and all the rest of it, but, apart from Hayden, they weren't told of Huntley's attack; they didn't know what I was going through.

Ben, my half-brother from my mother's first marriage, was trying to be a father-figure. 'You will do this because, if not, you will have me to deal with,' he would tell me. He had a controlling attitude and tried to force his will on me. I didn't want that.

I couldn't sneeze without him being there and telling me off for it. One time I was with my best friend Harriet at her house after my mum had punished me for doing one thing or another. I think it was for coming home half an hour or an hour late. This didn't happen that often because, if they said I had to be in by eight, then I would be in by eight, but this time she said, 'Right, you use this house like a hotel. You and Harriet can go to her mum's house.'

Because Harriet's mum didn't have much money, she couldn't afford to buy us drinks or food or anything like that, and all due respect to Harriet's mum, because she was a nice lady, but we both more or less lived on toast. I used to think, Oh God, I'm starving.

I would go back home and I would say to my mum, 'I've only had two slices of toast today.'

Her punishment was to say, 'You go there, you live the way you want to live. You go and stay there.'

And I would reply angrily, 'Right, OK.'

When I came back to stay temporarily, my mum's brother, Uncle Kev, said, 'I'll treat you lot to Skegness.' He was offering to take us to see his son, my cousin Jordan, sing on stage.

That would be fantastic, I thought. But Mum laid down one proviso, telling me, 'Yes, that's fine, as long as you are good.'

Harriet and I got dressed nicely and did our hair, nails and make-up. We came down the stairs and I went to the fridge, took out two Penguin bars and offered one to Harriet.

'What are you doing?' said the ever-vigilant Ben.

I started to give him a running commentary. 'I'm just having a chocolate bar...'

'No you are not,' he interrupted. 'You can put that back.'

I was taken aback by his immature pettiness. 'Excuse me, I'm hungry,' I shot back, 'and I'm having a chocolate bar. You don't even live here.' At that time he had his own house.

'Put it back now,' he ordered loudly.

So I did, but I made my anger clear, insisting, 'But I'm hungry.'

He sounded like Mum when he accused me, 'You use this house like a hotel.'

I said, 'Why, because I go out to work on Thursday, Friday and Saturday nights? It's not like I'm going out and standing on a street corner.' I was waitressing at a pub on those evenings, but more about that later.

This Penguin incident developed into a full-blown argument. At the dining table Ben kept winding me up so that I lost my patience and snapped at him. Still he wouldn't stop. He was having a go at me in front of Harriet. If I complained to Mum or Dad about things like this, they would just say, 'Well, don't wind him up then.' It wasn't a case of pulling the dog's teeth: it was more a case of avoiding the dog in the first place.

When Uncle Kev arrived, he asked, 'Has Ben been having a go at you again?'

'Yes,' I told him.

In fact, my uncle had just walked past the conservatory and seen what was going on, so he said to Ben, 'Leave her alone.'

'Shut up,' the usually mouthy Ben croaked weakly.

With my brother Hayden, it was like a love/hate relationship and Adam still called me names, but not as much as the rest of them.

If I were to get the milk out of the fridge, pour it in a glass, put it down and just leave the carton there for a minute while I drank this milk, he would order, 'Get that lid back on that milk and stick it back in the fridge, you lazy little sod.'

'I was just going to drink it and then pour some more in. I'm dying of thirst,' I would say.

'Get it back in the fridge, now,' he would bleat relentlessly.

He used to taunt me, call me names like 'you little bitch', but it was more a case of 'I will control you and you will do as I say'. It seemed that they all wanted some control over me, including Huntley. I think the more inferior a man feels, the more he wants to exert control over anyone he deems to be weaker than him.

So you can see how things were at home. No wonder I never knew what real love was until I met Colin. I'd tried to escape all that at 13 by running away from home. I ended up living in an open house with about six lads and eight girls. I knew all of the lads and most of the girls because they were Hayden's friends. I would like it to be known that there was no sexual involvement between any of the boys and me. They were more like how brothers should be, because they looked out for me. They were there with their girlfriends. I was just using that space to clear away family cobwebs, to escape problems at home.

I lived there and I thought it was fine; I knew people who lived in that surrounding area, and I hoped to work at McDonald's. Even though I was only 13, I wanted to get a job and claim my independence. I knew these girls that worked at McDonald's, but I couldn't get hold of them and for about four days I didn't have anything to eat. I was literally starving and there was no food whatsoever in the house.

There was never food in the house. Well, there was one tin of macaroni cheese that one of the girls bought for me. We had to get a knife and cut the tin open, and then heat the stuff up in a bowl in the microwave, as we didn't have a cooker. I got one tin of that a week for about a month, and that is what I lived on. I was desperate, trying to think of ways I could get some money for something to eat.

One day, I went into the local shop, baseball cap on – you weren't allowed to wear baseball caps in that shop, but they could have seen I was a girl – and in my best grown-up voice I asked, 'Twenty Richmond Superkings, please.'

'Yes, certainly,' they said and put the packet down in front of me.

I went through the motions of getting money out of my pocket, but then grabbed the fags and did a runner. Afterwards, I thought, Shit!, because I knew there was no need for it. I felt absolutely shit, and sorry for the shopkeeper.

Not long after that, I saw Hayden and he had a message, 'Mum wants to meet up with you in McDonald's tomorrow at 12.'

'Yeah, all right then,' I said.

So she rolled up, which I thought was a good opportunity to sit down and try and sort something out sensibly and clear the air. She waltzed in with her friend, Dawn. I don't know how she had managed to become involved.

'Hiya,' I said to Mum.

She returned the greeting and gave me a look of concern. 'God, you look ill,' she remarked.

Sarcastically and without any fuss, I said, 'Well, you would, too, if you had to live off a tin of macaroni cheese a week.'

'Do you want a McDonald's?' she asked.

My stomach practically growled in response to the thought that I was about to have some food. I was dying to say yes, but all I could muster was a curt 'No thanks'.

I was almost kicking myself under the table, but I knew that as soon as she bought me that meal she would be trying to buy me back. No, I'm not having it, I thought. All the time I was sitting there, I was seeing these people eating chips. And then Dawn, sensing she was imposing, moved about in her seat uneasily and said, 'I'll leave you to talk. I'll go and get a coffee and bring it back.'

I thought Dawn would perhaps make herself scarce for ten minutes or so while we talked, but two minutes later there she was, trundling back towards us. I fumed to Mum under my breath, 'So we're supposed to sit here and talk about things openly and you brought your mate along. You wouldn't appreciate it if I brought my mate along, would you?'

Mum shifted her steely gaze away from me and answered awkwardly, 'No.'

My body language was screaming at my mum's friend to leave us alone. Casting her a hostile look, I asked, 'Exactly why are you here anyway, Dawn?'

She broke her silence with a barely audible, 'Well, your mum asked me to come along because she thought you were going to bring David Baxter.'

What is it with you and David Baxter? I thought as I replied, 'I don't want anything to do with him.'

Accusingly, Mum pointed her finger at me and said, 'You've been ringing him, because Hayden says.'

I took in her remark with open-mouthed disbelief, before replying, 'Yes, and Hayden is a bullshitter, because that's not the case. I haven't. Yes, I've got his number, but I haven't got credit on my phone to ring.'

Just as I had felt disbelieved by everyone over the Huntley attack, here was my mum bolstering my doubt in her even more. She threw another knife into my heart with her sharp words: 'I don't believe you.'

At that point, I thought we were going to have a full-blown argument, but all of a sudden she was all nicey-nicey. 'Do you want to come home?' she asked me.

Sensing the lack of love, I said, 'No.'

As if I was some down and out, Mum sullenly asked, 'What are you going to do?'

'I'm going back to the place where I'm staying and I'm fine, don't you worry,' I told her. 'You get on with your life and I'll get on with mine.'

Dawn, trying to be the emissary of peace, made an impassioned plea. 'Hailey, come home. Come back, don't be silly.'

'No,' I spat. 'I may be frigging starving, filthy, no clean clothes – I have worn the same clothes for a month, but they have been washed every single night, you know. Hand-washed. They may have been washed with Fairy Liquid and not proper detergent like you use, but I'm fine. You know, without all the material things, I'm a lot happier than I used to be at home.'

I believe that meeting at McDonald's was nothing more than a spying mission on my mum's part to see if I had been in touch with my dad, and that was the fear that drove her to meet me – nothing else. Her fear was that I might have told him about family life but I made my feelings clear, telling her, 'I don't want anything to do with him. I've washed my hands of him. I've got my own life, right, OK?'

That little sermon said, I got up, walked out without casting my mum a fond or even worried farewell glance and went back to the open house. The fixation my mother had with David Baxter escaped me. Why she had to accuse me of being in contact with my biological father I do not know. I don't even want to examine what it was all about, although, down the line, my path would cross with David Baxter's.

So I was back at the open house. I felt really guilty about not having any money to contribute to the house, to which they would say, 'We don't care, you're all right.' But, I had about two of those fags I'd run off with and gave the rest to the others because, I explained, 'I can't pay you anything.' And they told me, 'Don't be daft.'

The lad whose place it was was really nice and if anybody knocked on the door he would come down the stairs – I was sleeping in the front room – and he would say, 'Don't worry, Hailey, I'm just going to see who that is at the door.'

Although the people living there were on drugs, they were not taking drugs from early in the morning until last thing at night. They would just have a few joints and a drink. It was that sort of environment, but where else could I stay? That was the first time that I tried speed. You put it in a Rizla paper and 'neck' it: drink it down with something fizzy. Every night I couldn't feel it doing anything to me, but they would say, 'Well, your eyes are a bit wide open.' And obviously I couldn't get to sleep, because that is what amphetamine does to you. The following morning I would wake up feeling like absolute crap and a bit disappointed.

About a week or two after that dire meeting with my mum at McDonald's, I saw Hayden and he told me,

'Mum wants you to go home so she can talk to you.'
He said something along the lines of: 'Mum has got
some money for you at home. She wants to speak to
you. Go to the house, nobody's in.'

He gave me the keys and I set off. I walked all the
way from Cleethorpes to Humberston. From where I
was staying, near the train station, it was a good couple
of hours' walk. I had my size-five Rockport shoes on.
I'm a size six, and halfway my feet were killing me, so I
ended up walking the rest of the way barefoot. Talk
about the return of the prodigal.

Anyway, I got home and discovered I'd lost the keys,
so I tentatively knocked on the door, expecting Mum
to answer. When one of my brothers opened up, I was
knocked for six and my heart missed a beat. No sooner
had I stepped inside the house and the door was closed
behind me than he started to have a go at me.

'You've been on drugs. You've run away from home,'
he accused me.

'Yes, I have, and I'm not going to deny it. Yes, I have,'
I answered.

'You little bitch, I hate you. You little cow! I'm going
to have you,' he blasted.

As frightened as I was, I managed to say, 'Listen, I've
come to sort it out with Mum. I'm sorry if I've caused
any heartache or what have you.'

'Don't give me that. You'll do the same next month,'
he said.

'No, no, I won't,' I promised. I was so scared of him I would have said anything to talk my way out of it.

'Just go to your room,' he roared

But I stayed downstairs with him while he ranted and raved at me for about half an hour.

I just sat there in tears, thinking, You bastard, I hate you. Then, retaliating, I shouted, 'I'm going to kill you one day.'

When my mum came in, my brother couldn't wait to spill the beans. 'She has just said that she is going to kill me, she is going to knife me and she is going to stick a knife in my back when I am asleep.'

I exploded, 'No. I just said, "I am going to kill you."'

'I'm having the police, Mum. I'm going to have the police,' he said.

'If you want to call the police, you call the police,' my mum told him.

'Good. I've about had it now and I'm pissed off,' I shouted. 'If you want to call the police, you call the police, mate.'

'Well, what's been going on?' Mum asked.

When I explained to her, she had the nerve to tell me, 'You shouldn't be winding him up then. You've only got yourself to blame.'

I was stunned by her refusal to see the reality of the situation. 'Oh, for God's sake,' I said to her. 'I've just come home to try and make it up with you. You're saying that you want to speak to me, me and you on our own, and then, when I arrive, he is here and he lays into me. He's very good; he knows what he is doing with it.'

All I got again was: 'You shouldn't wind him up. You've only got yourself to blame.'

The police were never called, and that was that. For the time being, I remained at home despite the shitty atmosphere.

In a merry-go-round of being kicked out and returning home, I found myself constantly saying sorry, then she would kick me out again and the cycle would repeat itself. It was like being attached to a yo-yo, but it was my mum's ego that I was connected to. She was a control freak and I was her fix.

Eventually and inevitably, it all came to a head when I was 15. Right, enough is enough, I thought. Both my parents used to manipulate my friends' parents by saying, 'It's Hailey that is naughty. It's Hailey that is on drugs.' I wasn't on drugs every day or even every six months. We used to get into a group and smoke it. Feeling peer pressure, I thought, Well, I've got nothing to lose, I'll go for it. I was scared when I took it. What happens if I die? I thought. But I enjoyed it and carried on smoking it, though I would only have a drag of it like a cigarette.

I didn't drink every single day. I used to earn my money from my evening waitressing job and go down the local shop, where the lady used to serve me with my alcohol and say, 'As long as you are sensible with it, then I don't care.' She was really nice, but I suppose I would have thought that because she was selling me booze. Friends of 16 or 17 were stopping me and saying, 'Hailey, will you go and get me such and such?'

I never asked her for spirits, because then she would have stopped serving me for taking the mick. I would only want four tins of lager or some alcopops. I never used to get so totally off my face that I ended up in hospital, not once. I would have a drink and, most of the time, when I came back you wouldn't know that I'd been drinking. Mind you, you could tell I'd been drinking when I was on the way home, because my friends and I would be laughing and joking all the time. But as soon as I got home, I would go straight to my room.

8

A F★★★★G LITTLE SLAPPER
AND A WHORE

As I got older, I started feeling more secure, safer and stronger in myself. I would think, No, I don't need to cut my arms and I don't need to take overdoses and try and kill myself. I would think, Well, I am here whether anybody likes it or not, so I might as well live life to the full. I was fed up with people calling me horrible names and insulting me. 'Look at you, you have got a sweating problem' or 'I heard that Hailey wets the bed' – things like that. Somehow I managed to pull myself together, and I put a lot of my progress down to my part-time waitressing job. I'd started this, working just on Sundays at first, when I was 14.

The job, at the Coach House pub, in Humberston, needed very little in the way of academic skill, but it brought me on a lot and slowly I started to come out of my shell. I was happy for the first time in a number of years, working for the landlady there, and she paid me £30 a shift.

I worked hard and I felt quite proud because I had a bit of responsibility. I took a first tentative step towards looking after myself properly by going out to buy some make-up and a pair of jeans that looked nice. I even surprised myself when I demoted the trainers of my brother's that I'd been wearing and took to high-heeled shoes. Then I decided I wanted to have my hair permed and to let it grow long again.

But, although the job was restoring my confidence, I was still having trouble at home. One evening I was getting ready to go to work, and I put on my black trousers and my white shirt and tied my hair up in a bobble. I did my make-up and, even though I say it myself, I looked really nice. Sorry if that comes across as 'I love myself', but it was better than being self-deprecating, as I had been for so long up until then. Anyway, one of my brothers came up to me and we started arguing. He ended up pushing me on to a chair, which broke into what seemed like a million pieces. I was on my back across this chair and he had me by the scruff of my neck. I can't remember what the argument was about, but it kicked off with him calling me a little bitch and accusing me of things. All I could say was: 'I haven't done anything wrong.'

So many times I got punished for something that I'd never done. That evening I got to the pub 20 minutes late and the landlady asked, 'Hailey, are you all right?'

Even though I had make-up on my white shirt and my hair was bedraggled, I told her, 'Yeah, I'm fine, thanks.'

'Has one of your brothers had a go at you again?' she asked in a knowing way.

'Yeah,' I answered meekly.

She tried to bolster my confidence and said, 'Don't worry about it.'

I felt totally crap, but, as soon as I was serving meals, people would be saying, 'Thanks ever so much.' The praise from these patrons of the pub was a great boost. I was receiving praise from total strangers; praise that I needed but wasn't getting at home.

I'd been in contact with social services a few years earlier, of course, but I wasn't receiving any help from them now. I was on my own – a lost soul. Here I have to give credit to the children's charity ChildLine. At this stage, I used to ring them about four times a week and they gave me really helpful advice, as well as great solace and reassurance. In fact, the lady on the phone was so nice that I used to think, I wish I could come and live with you; you are a nice person and you don't shout and you don't grab people by the scruff of their neck.

No one from social services gave me follow-up support. It's talked about a lot but I don't think this sort of support exists as much as people would like to think or the media portrays. Social workers always say, 'We have learned from our mistakes' or 'We have had a valuable lesson and it won't happen again.' How many times have we heard this? It's just a euphemism for: 'Sorry, we fucked up and we're covering our arses by saying the words you want to hear us say.'

I began to work at the pub on Thursday, Friday and Saturday evenings from about seven o'clock until midnight or one o'clock in the morning. After my shift, the landlady would drive me home or she would call a taxi for me. Saturday was just glass collecting, cleaning ashtrays and tasks like that. The landlady also showed me how to pull pints and use the till, so I started doing this too. I looked much older than I was and would quite easily have passed for someone in their late teens.

By now I wasn't going to school any more. I had been expelled in bizarre circumstances. There was a break-in at the school and a video recorder had been stolen. Rumours were going around that I and two other girls were responsible.

It was true, but for three weeks I said nothing to anybody about it. Mum and Dad had been told that I was involved, but nothing was said to me until I came home after school one night and my mum broached the subject. 'You have been quiet, Hailey,' she said. 'I've spoken to PC Woods and asked him to come round tomorrow.'

To cut a long story short, I said to her, 'I'm going to tell him that I stole the VCR with these two girls.'

Feigning surprise with a holier-than-thou look, she asked, 'Oh. Why?'

'Well, there's no denying it. I have done it,' I replied.

'Oh, no, Hailey,' she said. 'You're a fool. It will go on your record.' She wasn't very happy with me.

I confessed to PC Woods, 'Look, three weeks ago the school got broken into, a video recorder got stolen. It was two of my friends and me.'

Without any ceremony, he said, 'You are under arrest.'

At the police station, I found that the other two girls had been brought in and they said to me, 'Why did you want to admit it?'

I think the police and my mum colluded in trying to teach me a lesson. The idea was: 'Put her in the cells for a while and she won't do it again.' So they kept me locked up from about nine in the morning until about five in the afternoon and then I was given a warning and sent home. I was also grounded for about a month, and during that month I was suspended from school.

I was called back to the school with my mum for a meeting with the headmaster. 'Why did you do it?' I was asked.

'I just hate school,' I answered. In reality, though, I loved it because there were people that I knew and it was somewhere I could escape to. 'I really don't like coming,' I lied.

By now, Mum was practically crying and said to the headmaster, 'Please don't expel her from school. The guy that used to live down the road from us sexually abused her in the school grounds.'

What I couldn't grasp was how she felt able to use the allegation about Huntley to exploit being sexually abused on my behalf. I look back and wish she had kicked up more of a fuss and dug her heels in and believed me more. Had she trusted my word more then, she could have gone to the press, or even stuck posters up in the neighbourhood or put leaflets through everybody's door. But now she was using my ordeal as a reason for me not to be expelled.

As far as the break-in was concerned, I said, 'I'm sorry. I'll pay for any damage and I'll pay for the broken window. I'll pay for the VCR and if there is any damage I'll pay for a new one.'

I put my honesty before anything else, and that should prove I am not a liar. Besides, I thought, if I admit it now, I won't get in as much trouble, rather than leave it and find six weeks down the line that they know it was me because of CCTV footage. That would have been far worse.

By this time, Mum had bought a house in Cleethorpes, an old police house that she had moved into with Wayne and that they were doing up. She had somebody come and tile the floor for her because she didn't know how. They were there for about two or three days, and there was nobody in the house apart from these two guys and me.

I said, 'Can I make you a cup of tea or anything?'

One of the tilers asked for two sugars, but made a thing about it, saying, 'Two sugars, please, but don't stir it because I don't like it sweet.' I was looking at him rather confused. You don't like it sweet, I thought, so why do you have sugar in it in the first place?

'It's all right,' he chirped. 'I'm just winding you up.'

'All right then,' I replied.

So I made them some tea and, because nobody else was in the house, I spent all day sitting there talking to them and making them cups of tea.

Later that day, there were some other builders at the side of the house putting in a window. My brother Ben had come in earlier and one of them remarked to him, 'I bet you enjoy coming here every now and again?'

'Why?' Ben asked.

This builder went on about spying on me and my brother said, 'She's not my sister, she's a fucking little slapper and a whore. I fucking hate her.

He wasn't saying all this openly in front of me, as I was in the kitchen at this point. He told the builder, 'She's just a little slapper and she takes drugs. What a whore she is. We don't like her. She treats this house like a hotel.'

It was a regular complaint of his. Admittedly, I *did* use the house like a hotel. But between seven and pub closing time on Thursday, Friday and Saturday nights I was getting off my backside and working. Not a lot of

15-year-olds do that, because they get their mum and dad to pay for everything, but I didn't want that.

My knight in shining armour was Colin, who had heard the conversation and now said to Ben, 'You're the fat kid at school that nobody likes, aren't you?'

My brother was taken aback. 'Sorry?'

Colin had a face like thunder as he said, 'I have sat and watched Hailey, and she is a really nice girl and she has been making us cups of tea. You are the fat bastard at school that nobody likes and you can only pick on your sister.'

In a desperate attempt to deflect this attack, Ben could only come up with: 'Don't talk to your employer like that!'

'Listen, mate,' Colin told him, really angry by now, 'you are *not* my boss and, as soon as this floor is finished and I get paid, I'm off.'

The next thing, Ben left, and soon afterwards, when the tiling was all done, I helped the guys mop the floor. Now I said to Colin what I had meant to say before Ben came in: 'Why don't you pop in for a drink at the Coach House one night?'

'Yeah,' he said.

'I work there on Thursday, Friday and Saturday nights and sometimes on a Monday,' I explained.

When Colin came into the pub, I pulled him a pint and we got talking. I looked mature for my age and he thought that, because I was serving people alcohol, I had to be 18 or more, and didn't ask how old I was. No one in the pub mentioned anything about my age to him. And I wasn't about to say I was only 15, as the pub would have got into trouble for employing me. This explains why later Colin was to be charged with unlawful sexual intercourse.

One night, there was a rare family do when Mum, Hayden and me went to a pub called Shoeberts in Cleethorpes. Mum had asked some friends and family to come along. Auntie Bet was there with her granddaughter Leanne, and my brother Adam rolled up. He and Leanne ended up going out to a nightclub, and later on she told me that they had sex.

I was sitting there in the pub when Colin walked in. This time I didn't really look at him twice. I sat drinking with Mum and then, as it dawned on her that Colin was there, she exclaimed, 'Oh my God, that's my tiler. That's Colin. Come and have a drink, Colin.'

'I'll buy them,' Colin said, and bought everybody a drink. Then my mum bought him a drink and said, 'Why don't you come back to ours for a coffee?'

'No, no, I am all right,' he said.

By this time, I had changed my mind and taken rather a liking to Colin. I went to the toilet and, when I came out, opportunely we ran into each other. But, when I asked him to call me, he looked at me as if I was playing with him.

9

KISSED FOR THE VERY FIRST TIME

At this stage I was unaware that Colin was separated from his second wife and that he had two children by his first wife, two boys.

A couple of days went by before he called me. When I heard his voice, my heart almost missed a beat. 'Hiya, it's Colin here,' he said. 'Hope you're OK. Hey, was this a wind-up the other night, you giving me your phone number?'

Without having planned it, I said, 'To be honest, I was wondering if I could take you out for a drink sometime.'

'Yes,' he said, then, 'Are you *sure* this isn't a wind-up?'

'No,' I reassured him. 'Look, if you want to take me for a drink sometime, then let me know.'

'Yeah, all right,' he said.

I still didn't think he believed I was being serious.

Anyway, we ended up having a few drinks and I was really beginning to like him. As we got to know each other better, over drinks and meals, Colin introduced me to his friends and all the local pubs. Then, before long, people I knew myself were seeing us together.

As I began to trust Colin more, what had happened to me in my life just came out. He didn't bat an eyelid, but he did say that he'd suspected all was not well when he saw me moping about the house when he was working for my mum. To be honest, I think it would have been obvious to a lot of people that my life had caved in.

'Why don't you move out?' Colin suggested.

I still hadn't revealed my age. I couldn't very well say I was still a schoolgirl, so I told him that, as I hadn't got the deposit for a house and I couldn't afford to rent a place, I was just going to have to stay at my mum's house until I could save up some money for a deposit.

It was the summer of 2001 and I was permanently excluded from school on 28 June, having turned 15 that April. Colin was 34. At that stage, we had more of a friendship than anything else. One night, when we'd been seeing each other for a couple of months, we were in the pub and I told him about my mum, about how I didn't get on with her and the love/hate relationship we had.

That same evening, I plucked up the courage and told Colin about that bastard Huntley. Taken aback at my determination to get justice, he said, 'You wouldn't think you had been through that, to look at you.'

It was ten to six as we strolled towards the car, and I thought, I'll be in for about seven. Not that I had to be in for then. We lingered around talking and wondering whether to go somewhere else for another drink. Then my phone started ringing.

I answered it and Mum's unmistakable voice said, 'It's only me.'

'Are you all right?' I asked.

'Yes,' she said, and then, 'Whereabouts are you?'

'I'm in Cleethorpes,' I told her.

At this she went mad and shouted, 'Get your fucking arse home, *now!*'

'What's the matter?' I asked defensively.

'Just get home *now,*' she barked.

As Colin was there, I summoned up my best behaviour and asked her, 'Look, what is all this about? Just tell me.'

Colin heard both sides of the conversation because I was standing right next to him, so I said to him, 'I'm not bullshitting, this is what she is like.'

Then Mum started going on about my biological father, David Baxter. Hayden had mentioned to me that he had seen our real dad and, curious, I'd asked what he was like.

'Why don't you come along and meet him?' he said. I accepted his invitation.

At that time, Hayden wanted to go and live with his father, which is why Mum was on the phone to me now: she was under the impression that I was with David Baxter and that I wanted to live with him too.

She went on, 'Get back home. I'm going to pack your bags and they'll be in two bin bags out the front, in two minutes. So you better get home now.'

'It's going to take me ten minutes to get home,' I said.

'If you are not home in two minutes, your bags are going to be packed,' she threatened.

Feeling abandoned, I tried to call her bluff by saying, 'In that case, pack my bags then, but I've done nothing wrong. You're shouting on about David Baxter.'

'You want to live with David Baxter,' she yelled.

'No I don't,' I said guardedly.

'Yes you do,' she replied.

'Well, even if I did, I don't even know him,' I countered.

'If you ever come back to this house, I will fucking do this and I will fucking do that,' she threatened me.

Colin was standing there listening and the bewilderment on his face told me what he was thinking. Apologetically, I said, 'I told you what she was like from the start. I don't want to go back there.'

As luck would have it, he was moving to Hull in the next three days because his family were there. 'Feel free to come with me if you like,' he offered. 'Go and get your stuff from the house and give your mum your keys.'

I tried to stifle the alarm that must have been written on my face at the prospect of going home and saying, 'I'm moving out today, even though I'm only 15.'

I couldn't go back home and give my mum the keys because I didn't have any of my own. And if I were to pack my clothes she would demand to know where I was going.

'I'm not going back there,' I told Colin. 'I don't care. She can throw out all my possessions.'

That night we stayed in a hotel and the next day we drove over to Hull, where I met Colin's family. We ended up renting a house in Clyde Street. It was like the Bronx, but we couldn't afford anywhere better.

Colin started working in a fish factory and I started working in a gift shop, pricing gifts. I was being paid £30 a day, cash in hand. Colin was on a weekly wage.

After a couple of weeks, we were starting to get into a routine, but during that time my mum had made no efforts to contact me.

Colin would pick me up from the shop after work, and one day when he turned up, quite out of character, he asked me coldly, 'Is everything all right?'

I gave his steady eyes a searching gaze. I was looking for a telltale sign of what was wrong as I said, 'Yes.'

'What's the matter?' he probed. 'You seem to be a bit

quiet and a bit distant. Was it that meal we had last night? Was it no good?'

Lost in my thoughts about what he could be getting at, I replied touchily, 'No, no, no, it was fine.'

When Colin's brother came round to our house later that evening, he asked me, 'How are you, all right?'

'Yes,' I said.

I knew in that split second that something was going to come out about my age. Then Colin asked me, 'Is there anything you want to tell me?'

'No,' I said, on my guard now.

'Are you sure?' he pressed.

'Yes,' I insisted.

Colin looked at me and asked again, 'Are you sure you have got nothing that you want to say?'

I brazened it out once more, saying, '*No*, nothing whatsoever.'

Pain was etched across his face as he opened a newspaper and then put it down in front of me. The headline read: 'Bring my daughter home, she is only 15'. Beneath it was a big picture of me when I was 12.

My mum wasn't telling me to come home: she was asking for her daughter to be brought back home... to a home she had told me not to come back to.

She had checked her phone bill and seen that I had been calling Colin from the house. And it was equally clear to her that Colin had parted from his wife before he had met me. Somehow his wife knew that he was seeing somebody called Hailey. This much my mum had found out.

So this plea for me to be returned home that was plastered across the newspapers had already been put to the police. It turned out that they had advised my mum, 'Don't go to the press,' but she had gone ahead and done just that.

I started crying and blubbered to Colin, 'Look, I'm so sorry; I know I've landed you in a load of crap. I'm so sorry, I didn't mean it to come out like this.'

'Why did you lie to me?' Colin croaked, a confused look on his face.

He couldn't understand why I said that I was 19 when I was 15, but all I could say was: 'All this crap that was going on at home was bad and then I got feelings for you.'

I'd known he felt the same but if I'd said, 'Oh, by the way I'm only 15,' he would have gone, 'Ta, ta.' Never in a month of Sundays would he have said, 'Oh, OK.'

'That's why I never mentioned it,' I told him.

My going missing as a minor caused a nationwide alert that I had been abducted. And, because it was big news, Colin's solicitor called to find out if I was the missing Hailey and Colin confirmed that I was.

'Listen, come in and see me,' the solicitor said. We went to his office and he said, 'What we need to do is this: I will come with you to the police station and you hand yourselves in and explain what has gone on and we will get things sorted out.'

I felt really bad and I was thinking, Why did I lie about my age? I knew that, if Colin had known I was only 15, he would have gone, 'Right, nice meeting you, see you later,' but of course he had no idea.

The solicitor told us that there was nothing that could be done that night. Instead, he advised us to go back home and said that we should come back to his office first thing in the morning and he would drive us to the police station in Grimsby.

He had already made the appointment and Colin's sister-in-law had already called the police to confirm, 'Colin is here with me and Hailey is with him. We are coming in tomorrow morning.'

When we arrived, there were about 50 uniformed officers standing outside the police station. Someone must have been selling tickets!

We ran the gauntlet of hate and managed to squeeze into the building. I walked in first and Colin followed. One of the policemen greeted us sarcastically, 'Now then, Colin, your time's up. We knew we would catch you one day.'

If only they had deployed half this mob against Huntley, things might have ended differently.

Anyway, Colin stood up for himself and said, 'Nobody has caught me, mate. I'm handing myself in. I can explain what this is all about.'

Well, the good old social services that had blundered and let me down in the past had spotted the newspaper articles about me and come running. Where were they when I was all but dumped by everyone? So they were in on this one for the easy ride, reuniting a lost soul with her family.

I don't particularly care how social services became involved. Who wants a load of lesbian Marxists chasing after them? I think they were called in by a police officer before our meeting. Anyway, they called my mum at home and after all her chasing about after me and all her crocodile tears she said cheekily to them, 'Don't bother sending her back here, because she has caused too much trouble.'

I was incensed and thinking, Yesterday you were pleading in the papers, 'Bring my daughter home, I love my special daughter so much,' and now that I am actually back in Grimsby, now I am here, you don't want me back home.

Anyway, I ended up staying with the landlady of the Coach House, Mandy Addison, first at her mum's house, which she was looking after while her mum was on holiday, and then at the pub. The night we returned to the pub we'd just had a pizza and a bottle of WKD, a Vodka-based drink, when it was bang, bang, bang at the door. Mandy's boyfriend got up to answer it and I was shaking because I was already a bag of nerves.

It was a policeman, and he tested my patience to the

limit when he said, 'Excuse me, Hailey. Come over here. Sorry, you have to come with me, but you shouldn't even be here. You've run away from home for the second time.'

My ears couldn't believe what that callous woman, my mum, had done. She had lodged another complaint that I was a runaway and she wanted me back at home. Her Jekyll and Hyde character was beginning to piss me off, and the revs were off the clock, as Colin would say.

'No, I haven't run away!' I protested. 'I've been staying here for a week. I'm staying here now.'

But the policeman insisted, 'No, you're not. Your mum wants you home.'

Was I going loopy? I said, 'Hang on a minute; she didn't want me a week ago. I am not a rag doll that she can pick up when she wants me and put me down when she doesn't.'

My pleas were falling on the deaf ears of the law, as the officer just said, 'Yes, yes. Now get in that car, you're coming home with me.'

Mandy stuck up for me by saying, 'Now hang on, I have already spoken to Hailey's mum and she was champion for her to stay.'

To this, the policeman responded bombastically, 'No, she is not. She has said that Hailey has run away from home again.'

This was ludicrous, and all I can think is that my

mum was jealous that someone else was having the pleasure of my company. She didn't want David Baxter getting me, yet she threatened to chuck me out and said I should go and live with him.

Anyway, this policeman had a really shirty attitude and in the end he got me in his car. My mum had told the police to pick me up from the pub but she had also said they should take me to her brother's house, so I had to direct him to my Uncle Kev's place. Amazingly, she had the police doing her bidding as if they were her private army. I mean, if she had this much power now, what had gone wrong over the Huntley allegation? How come she hadn't been able to get them moving then? I'll tell you why: because she wanted her 15 minutes of fame, that's why.

We arrived at Uncle Kev's house around one in the morning, and I think he was aware I was coming. So there I was on his doorstep with my little rucksack.

At about nine o'clock the next morning, he said to me, 'Leave your rucksack on, get this helmet on and your coat, and jump on the back of my bike.'

'Why, where are we going?' I wanted to know.

'Just jump on,' he said in a reassuring tone.

Then I realised what this was all about. He knew Colin's sister-in-law, Michaela, was happy for me to stay with her because we had been talking about her earlier that morning.

'Well, if that is where you want to be, then that is

where you want to be,' he said to me. Michaela hadn't contacted Uncle Kev about the idea, nor had social services. He was acting on his own initiative.

'What's her address, by the way?' he asked.

I gave it to him and he said, 'Have you been on the back of a bike before?'

'No,' I replied hesitantly.

'Well, don't tell anybody we've done this,' he chuckled, adding, 'I would rather take you myself and know that you are safe rather than thinking that you will hitchhike or get the bus.'

Uncle Kev was a special constable, like my stepfather, and I was thinking, Not only are you a copper, but also you're my uncle. You're supposed to be saying, 'No, you will stay here.'

When we got to Michaela's house he came in with me to confirm that she was happy for me to stay there. She told him yes and that I would have her daughter's bedroom as she was moving out.

Later that day, Michaela rang social services and informed them, 'I've got Hailey here with me. She's happy for me to look after her and her uncle's happy for me to look after her.'

Social services said, 'She has got rights at 15, believe it or not, so she can stay where she wants to be, basically.'

I settled in, had my tea that night and then there was an ominous but familiar knock, knock, knock... There was a copper at the door again!

'Hailey?' he said.

Pretty pissed off with it all, I yelled, 'Yes!'

'We're just coming to check that the property is all right and that you're safe here,' he said.

With that, he got on his radio and said, 'Yes, I've got her here now. She is coming with me.'

'Have you not got anything better to do? I stormed. 'You can see that I am safe, I *am* being looked after. I *am* happier than I have ever been. Tell me, what problems am I causing? On Monday I am going to enrol at the college, and then when I am 16 I will carry on my relationship with Colin, if that is what he wants.'

This copper wouldn't listen. 'No, come with me, come with me,' he insisted.

Wearily I said, 'Right. OK then.'

As we walked out of the house, Michaela made a bit of fuss, saying, 'I've rung social services.'

It turned out that I was being taken back to the Coach House. It was all part of a plan that became clear the next day, a Sunday, when, bizarrely, David Baxter, my biological father, phoned the pub to make arrangements to pick me up, along with all my stuff.

I just can't, for the life of me, think how the police could apply so much effort and resources into rag-dolling me about from pillar to post. Anyway, the person my mum had been so fearful I'd end up living with was the very one I was going to be staying with now. And it was all because, for some reason, *she* had now involved him. To me, David Baxter was a complete stranger. I think I had only seen him once, when I was about 11. And that was for about ten minutes.

I felt in a worse position going with him than living in a halfway house. When he arrived at the pub he pompously announced, 'Young lady, get in this car. I am your father.'

I said, 'Listen, mate, let's get on the right foot here. Anybody can be a sperm donor, and anybody can put sperm into a cup and get somebody pregnant.'

Taken aback, he said warily, 'Right.'

I continued, 'And in my life, that's what you are. You weren't there for me to change my nappies, to take me out to the park, to take me fishing, swimming, anything like that. You were just not there and you never made any attempt.'

'Yes, I did. Yes, I did,' he defended himself pathetically.

I angrily retorted, 'No, you didn't, because you knew where I lived and you could have just banged on the door – "Right, Hailey. Hi, I'm your father" – instead of coming to collect me now, but you never did. You just totally blanked me.'

Visibly shaking, he responded feebly, 'I've got six other kids and to all these different women.'

I kept calling him 'Dave' or 'David'. He was miffed by this and said, 'I'm your father, young lady. I am not David, I am your dad.'

'No! That is where you are wrong,' I told him. 'Yes,

by law I am your daughter. But you are not my dad. I've got "Edwards" as my name. I was not happy there and I certainly am *not* going to be happy here.'

We arrived at his house and he said to me, 'This is my wife Anita, this is my son Daniel, and Anita's just had a baby called Emma.'

I just didn't want to know him. No, you have done nothing for me, I thought. I don't need you in my life, you are a stranger. At one point I was curious to see the plant that produced the seed I had grown from, to see what he looked like, but that was it.

The next morning he held his hand out and said, 'There's your pound.'

I should have remembered what my mum told me about strangers and, most of all, taking money from strangers. 'What's that for?' I asked.

Frostily, he barked instructions at me like a pantomime baddie. 'You walk down the road, you jump on the bus and then, when you finish college, you get off the bus and you come home.'

I was astounded by his flagrant lack of compassion as I asked, 'Where's the bus stop? How do I get there? Is it just one bus I need to get on? I mean, it's Burton upon Trent, it's like a big place. I don't know anybody.'

I set off and I was just about to get on this bus with 'College' displayed on the front. Which college, though? The fare was 80 pence and, as the driver didn't believe I was of school age, he classed me as an adult.

'No, I'm not, I'm off to the college,' I protested.

The power-crazed driver said, 'No, I'm sorry, I don't believe you. I'm going to charge you the full amount.'

I had 20 pence to my name. What was I going to get with 20 pence? I couldn't even afford the return fare.

During the day, *he* rang me. 'Now then, young lady, how are you?'

I gave him the same coldness back that he had earlier shown me. 'Oh, I'm great. Thanks for your generosity.'

He responded with mock-innocence, 'What do you mean?'

I stated the obvious. 'It cost me 80 pence on the bus to get here.'

'Right, don't worry about it. I'll pick you up after college, right?'

So I rang Colin with the 20-pence piece that I had and found out that he was working back at the fish factory in Hull. We were just chatting and then it all came out. I told him I was unhappy and he said, 'Just stick it out. Don't worry about it, you'll be fine. How's he treating you?'

'Like shit.'

'Oh.'

'I think a dog would get better treatment than me,' I said, and did an impression of David Baxter: 'Oi, get up here, young lady' and 'Do this.' 'I'm more like a skivvy to him, you know. I know what the future will hold for me here – I'll be looking after his kids whenever he wants to go out. I'll be like a prized possession on a Friday night with his workmates going, "This is my daughter," and "There you are, Hailey, have a Coke." Yeah, great.'

I remember when I first landed at David Baxter's house, for the first three or four days he gave me forty cigarettes a day. And then, on top of that, every time he would have a cigarette he would say to me, 'Here you are, do you want one?'

He smoked what seemed like three cigarettes every ten minutes and I was thinking, Go for it, fine by me. At the end of each day I had smoked the forty fags plus maybe ten more that he had dished out. Fine. But this went on for those three or four days only. After that I wasn't given any at all and I had to ask, 'Please, do you mind if I pinch a cigarette off you?'

'No,' came his terse reply.

Not amused, I asked, 'Why not?'

Self-importantly he said, 'Because, my way of teaching, you will learn a lesson.'

'What lesson is that then?' I said mockingly.

Seeing how he behaved, I could see where Mum had got her Jekyll and Hyde character: she was a mirror image of David Baxter. In an effort to piss me off and make me sick of smoking, he was trying aversion therapy on me. He tried, unsuccessfully, to psychologically break me. When I questioned him about why he wouldn't give me any cigarettes after his own version of Pavlov's dogs, the words he used were: 'I was hoping it would make you sick and you wouldn't want to smoke any more.'

After feeding me more than forty cigarettes a day for three or four days, he expected me to no longer need them. Backwards thinking, I say. But I bragged cheekily, 'It would take more than forty fags to make me sick. Bloody hell, you know that was a bit of a childish thing to do, wasn't it?' And I warned him, 'Listen, mate, Mum has tried it. She has been there, she has worn the T-shirt and I show her enough respect that I will not smoke in front of her.'

On my first Saturday there, I told him, 'I am off out.'

'Where are you going?' he asked in his obnoxious way.

I said, 'I'm off to Leeds with some friends from college who've got a car to do a bit of shopping.'

It was a cock and bull story. I had saved up a few 20-pence pieces from the change left over from the bus money, and I went to the pub and called Colin at the house we used to live in together. I told him I was going to Leeds for the day. But then I set off for his place, to give him a big surprise. Luckily, some friends of mine from college were going that way and gave me lift.

When I turned up on his doorstep he threw his arms up in despair. I was still 15 and his bail conditions meant he had to stay away from me. 'Oh, Hailey, we can't,' he implored me. 'You know, we're going to get into a load of trouble. Look, just try and stick it out until you are 16 and then you can do whatever you want.'

I was desperate too, about living with my father. 'I can't,' I said. With that, my phone rang (worst luck for me at this moment, although my phone was out of credit, it could accept incoming calls) and it was Baxter screaming obscenities down the line at me. 'Get home now!' he yelled.

'What's the matter?' I asked as smugly as I could.

'You're going wrong. I am not happy with you, young lady,' he said.

I took great delight in saying, 'Well, tell me what it is and we will resolve the problem.'

'Get home now!' he blasted back.

'I can't, I'm on my way to Leeds,' I lied.

'You can't be on your way to Leeds. Get home now,' he said, flying off the handle again. He knew that I had kept in touch with Colin and guessed correctly that I had gone to see him.

'No,' I shouted.

The snake had got himself all in a lather. 'I have looked through your diary and I know the house number in the street that you used to live in. I also know that you've been phoning Colin.'

I was furious that he had looked at my diary and I spat, 'There's nothing like respect around here, is there?'

Childishly, he said, 'I am not telling you what you have done wrong, but get home now.'

'No, just leave me to it and I will be home later on,' I said defiantly.

I was planning on going back about five o'clock that afternoon, after being with Colin.

For all his airs and graces of calling me 'young lady', Baxter went on swearing down the phone at me and telling me to get back at once. I switched the phone off. 'I'm not having anyone talking to me like that,' I said to Colin. 'I may be only 15, but that is shit the way he is talking to me.'

Colin tried to calm me down. 'What's the matter, darling?' he said.

But I was still raging. 'I don't know what I've done wrong. I've done something wrong and, if I have done it, fine, I will admit it and go, "Fine, sorry." There is nothing more I can do but say sorry.'

He soothed, 'Turn your phone back on and answer it and find out what the frigging hell is going on.'

As I switched my phone back on, it started ringing and, when I answered, Baxter said, 'Right, young lady, come home tonight. We will sit down, I'll buy you some White Lightning cider and a pizza and we'll talk about it.'

'Talk about what?' I asked. 'Tell me now, because there's nothing that is more annoying than trying to wind me up by saying that I have done something wrong and then trying to entice me to come back. Just tell me what I have done wrong.'

His true colours came out when he reached the end of his tether. 'You get home now or you'll end up back at your mother's, if I have my way.'

Colin's face was a picture of sadness as he said, 'You can't stay here because I am going to get into shit. I really want to help you but I can't.'

I thought, You're the one that I want to be with and people can see that, but they are not letting me. My feelings for Colin had been growing stronger and he cared a lot about me.

I wasn't going to go back to Baxter's. Instead, I went to Michaela's house and stayed there for a while. Colin had little to do with this, and Michaela rang social services and said, 'I'm just calling to let you know that Hailey is with me.'

I knew Colin and his family, and they respected me. This was the family that I wanted to be with. I knew that I would be looked after properly there. But nobody would let me do that.

By this time, Christmas wasn't far off and my mum rang and told me disdainfully, 'Hailey, I'm not having you staying away from me near Christmas. I'm not having any of my kids going without Christmas presents. If you and Colin want to come round, I don't care if Colin comes. Come round for Christmas dinner, that's fine, and then go back and do whatever you want to do. I'm not having any of my kids going without any Christmas presents.'

Well, to me Christmas comes but once a year. What about the other 364 days of the year?

'I don't want any presents,' I told her. 'No, no, no. I'm not falling into that one.'

I didn't feel like giving presents, or going there and having them say, 'There's your Christmas present.'

Then Michaela told me, 'I don't want anything coming back on us. I'm going to talk to social services again.'

'OK,' I said.

After the social workers had been round to talk to Michaela, they said they would be back in a week's time. True to their word, they returned, and they said, 'Right, you're going back to your mum's.'

I didn't kick or scream. I said to them, 'Look, I bet my bottom dollar, put a million quid on it that we get there and she will say, "No, you have caused too much pain and heartache to my family."' I knew this because she had already spoken to David Baxter while I was staying at his place and she had told him, 'I want our Hailey back because I want to get her a little flat or a little house, but I am not having her back here because she has caused too much upset in the family.'

I told the social workers, 'Well, if my mum was saying that to him and then telling the press, "Oh, I want my daughter back," then telling you that she doesn't want me back, she should make up her bloody mind.'

This is what she had told them. She was crying wolf and up to her old tricks. What was behind her behaviour, I think, was that she was trying to make my life damn uncomfortable.

I still kept in contact with her regularly, and told her, 'I'm safe, don't worry about me, I'm safe.'

Each time she would say, 'Right, fine.' She was talking to me with a little respect by now. But Ben, Adam and Hayden were still calling me 'bitch' and 'you little tart' and saying, 'You're a whore for running off with a 34-year-old man.'

And there were threats to Colin, like, 'I'm going to kick his face in when I see him.'

'Hang on a minute, he isn't the one that has done wrong here,' I would say.

I will admit, I shouldn't have lied to Colin about my age, but, if I hadn't gone through all the crap that I'd been through with my mum and dad, I would have had no reason to leave them. When I was living with them I had the latest TV and the latest computer and PlayStation, in my bedroom, a massive bedroom all to myself, with a double bed and anything that I wanted for the room. Materially, I wanted for nothing.

But, when it came to hugs and kisses or being taken for a day out, I was emotionally starved. 'Sorry, too busy,' they would say. I explained this to Mum and she said, 'You were always the belle of the house and you could have it.'

I said, 'No. That's not the case. I went without so that

your little blue-eyed boys could have everything that they wanted.'

I remember something happening when I was 15 that shows how little love and respect I was shown. I think I had about £2 and I wanted to go to the shop and buy a magazine.

'No, you're not going,' Dad barked at me.

'Why not?'

'Because I said so.'

Not letting the matter rest, I argued, 'The shop is only across the road, you can stand there and watch me, because I'm not going anywhere. I'll come back.'

'No, you are not. No, you are not, right?' he said. Here was another weak man wanting to dominate me.

We were doing up the house and a guy called Andy was hanging some doors for my mum. One of them was leaning against the wall and I was standing with my back to it, and my friend Harriet was standing at the other side of the room.

'For God's sake, Dad,' I raged. 'I'm off across the road to the shop. I'm not being rude, but I'm off to the shop. Don't you tell me what you are going to do.'

Whether he believed I was going to the shop or not, I didn't have a clue. We got into this big argument about me going to the shop. I was saying yes and he was saying no. He started screaming and shouting and giving me a lecture. That's when he lost a grip on his sanity and whacked me across my face.

This man has hands like shovels and it was full pelt. Harriet and Andy were really shocked at what they witnessed.

I started crying and then I went quiet. I went up to my bedroom and put on a CD that he didn't like: Eminem's album with all the swearing.

My adrenalin was surging. I was angry. I don't believe in a woman hitting a man or a man hitting a woman. You want to treat me like a bitch and you think that I am such a naughty little cow, I'll show you what one is, I thought. I had my windows open with the stereo on full blast, thinking, I don't care.

I stood there brushing my hair, getting ready to go out. My dad came into my bedroom. He had calmed down and he was thinking, Andy has just seen me smack my daughter in the face.

But then he shouted, 'Turn that shit off.'

I stood my ground and replied, 'No. You think I'm a naughty little sod and you can smack me in the face… then go for it. But I'm going to be a horrible little cow now. Then at least you've got a reason to smack me in the face.'

He was going on and on and on and I just lost it. 'Get out of my room,' I shouted, and chucked the hairbrush at him. When I was scared I used to shout and scream. I soon learned after the Huntley assault to use my vocal cords. I was scared now, and there was no other way that I could express my feelings apart from shouting, because my dad was a big man with a loud voice and built like you know what.

Harriet came upstairs and I said, 'Now can you see why I hate being here, because it's like this near enough every other day.'

'Do you want my honest opinion?' she said, because she was sensible.

'What?' I asked.

'I would leave. I wouldn't put up with that,' she told me.

By this time Dad had left the room and gone downstairs. When I went down he had gone out. Andy was hanging the doors and he asked, 'Crikey, are you all right?'

I told him, 'Nobody messes with me, you see. What goes around comes around.'

'What do you mean?' he asked.

'One day he'll be old,' I said. 'I mean, when he's a little frail 70-year-old man. He'll be going to the betting shop and some young thug as big as he was will land one on him. Then I'll have the upper hand. I don't need to go around hitting people to get my way.'

Andy asked me, 'Do you want a fag?'

'Yes, please,' I said gratefully.

So we had a fag and that was that. Nothing more was mentioned about it. When Mum found out, unlike when my dad had first hit me years earlier, she gave her usual couldn't-give-a-monkey's reply: 'Well, you shouldn't be messing about, you shouldn't be winding people up then, Hailey.'

I had become used to her and how she displaced the blame from the two of them to me. The truth was that I felt displaced by the needs of my brothers. I felt like the black sheep. Of course, the boys were like, 'I will protect you, Mum. Nobody will touch you, Mum, and if David Baxter comes round I will cave his head in.' Big mouths but nothing in their trousers to compensate when it came to action. They could talk the talk but not walk the walk.

Anyway, going back to the social services, when they came round the second time they said, 'We're going back to your mum's.'

I warned, 'Fine, have it your way, but she won't have me back.'

She may have made it crystal clear to social services that she wanted me back, and whinged on at the press and to the whole world, 'I want my daughter back.' But I knew differently.

These social workers, a man and a woman, seemed pretty clueless to me. They were like, 'Well, we understand it, Hailey, because, you know, you keep running away from home.'

'Excuse me, I didn't run away from home,' I corrected them.

No wonder they cock things up and end up in the

newspapers because of their incompetence. It was like the blind leading the blind. Social services were really no use to me and didn't pay any attention to my personal welfare. They just wanted my case off their books. I was just a 15-year-old girl out there, all alone.

Anyway, I ended up being taken to this house and I was left outside in the car and the idiot social workers said to me, 'We're going to lock the doors.'

I protested, 'No, you're not locking me in this car. You trust me that I am not going to do a runner. Here I am in a strange place, it's one o'clock in the morning and I don't know where I am. I'm not going to be running off anywhere, mate, because I don't know where I'm going.'

The male social worker moaned, 'Oh, Hailey, don't be so silly.'

'No, I think you are being pathetic locking me in this car,' I told him. 'If you want me to come with you, then I will come with you, but don't go locking me in any frigging car.'

Defeated, he replied, 'Right, OK, have it your way.'

I sat there and when they came back they confirmed what I'd predicted. 'We've made a call to your mum,' they said. 'She has said that she doesn't want you back. She doesn't want you because you have hurt the family and she has got to put her kids first.'

She had told them, 'No! I am not having her back. She does what she wants. I have washed my hands of her now.'

'Right, fine. She can have it her way,' I said.

After this, they took me to an orphanage in Queen's Parade, in Cleethorpes. They rolled up there and said inappropriately, 'Here's Hailey's report. She is a runaway.'

Social services in this country have a lot to answer for. I resented this tag and spat, 'I am *not* a runaway. My mum kicked me out of that house and said to me, "Don't bother coming back to this house, right?"'

So here I was, classified as a runaway. In reality, I was a tearaway. I have been let down on more than one account by more than one agency. I've been let down across the board.

I wish, looking back at how things have turned out between Colin and me, that my mum, who made such a fuss about our being together, had made half the fuss about what Huntley did to me. Yet nothing was done about that. The man that did hurt me and the man that did cause me so much damage and pain wasn't punished. But the man that was bringing me happiness and that I felt safe and secure with – Colin – has had all the flack.

So there I was, unwanted by my parents, dumped in this care home in the middle of the night. I had gone from being 'the belle of the house', as my mum claimed, to being a sexually abused outcast... damaged goods. Thanks, Mum.

10
KIDNAPPED AND TRAPPED

'WELL,' ASKED THE LADY IN THE CARE HOME, WHO HAD SOMETHING OF CRUELLA DE VIL ABOUT HER, 'HAVE YOU HAD SOMETHING TO EAT?'

'I'm not hungry,' I snapped.

She replied coldly, with all the grace of a concentration camp commandant, 'Well, if you don't have something to eat now, it will go on to your report.'

'What report?' I asked.

Taunting me, she replied, 'You will have to be force-fed if you don't eat for a certain amount of time.'

I decided to meet this ice queen halfway by saying, 'No, I'll eat in the morning,' but it was something like one o'clock in the morning now.

My compromise seemed to have melted some of her

coldness away, and she said, 'Well, as long as you eat breakfast in the morning, then.'

'Right, OK then,' I said.

She told me where my room was and warned me, 'Mind, take your bag with you, lock the door and make sure none of the other kids come down and nick your stuff.'

By this time I was thinking, Well, I've got nothing to take, really. All I owned in the world was a pair of trousers.

Morning soon arrived and there was a lot of hustle and bustle as everyone was going out. One would say, 'I am off to my singing lesson,' and another, 'I am off to my ballet lesson.' What a perfect little life you have got, I thought. I know it sounds horrible, but there was this little girl there, really posh, and she said, 'I'm off to my dancing lesson. Would you like to come?' Just shut up, I was thinking, as in reality I was oozing with jealousy.

These were a carer's own children, and they were going to their dancing lessons. I was wishing that I could just be normal, like going swimming on a Saturday.

I brushed my teeth, cleaned round my room, took my bag and locked my door. I was still thinking hard when one of the carers said to me, 'Hailey, what are you doing today?'

'Can I go out?' I asked. 'I've never been in one of these places before. Are you allowed to leave the premises or are you held prisoner, sort of thing?'

She shook her head frantically from side to side as she

replied, 'No, no, we couldn't do that, because you can ring the police and say that we're holding you hostage. No. You can go out. Once a week we give you pocket money, £9.'

It was all falling into place. 'Right,' I said. So they could force-feed you but weren't allowed to keep you prisoner. Very strange.

She asked, 'Would you like yours next week or now? Because if you have it next week you can have £18, but if you want it now you can have £9.'

Holding in my excitement at the prospect of being able to leave the place and being paid to do so, I replied casually, 'I'm going to go to my friend's and she only lives around the corner. I want to take a video with me and we could watch that and have a pizza.'

'Have your £9 now, then,' she said. 'But take your stuff with you, though, Hailey, because I don't want anybody going in your bag and nicking it.'

I was on cloud nine as I replied, 'Yeah. OK. Put my stuff in my bag, right. See you later.'

As I sauntered out of the door, her voice trailed off as she said, 'Right. Remember, be back for curfew at five o'clock.'

I had the stare of a fashion mannequin as I said, 'OK, yeah.'

On the bus from Grimsby to Hull, I ended up drinking. Knock, knock, knock... I was back at Colin's house. He told me to go back to Michaela's, so I went there and I ended up staying, and she called social services again. I didn't return to the care home.

I expected to go through the pillar-to-post scenario again, as Michaela phoned social services to tell them I was back at her place.

Then, in the local corner shop near Colin's house, there was a poster on display with the heading 'WANTED FOR KIDNAPPING' and a photograph of Colin's face. I found out from Michaela that Colin had gone into this shop and asked, 'Who put that up there?'

'This woman with short dark hair,' came the reply. That description fitted my mum.

'Take it down,' Colin demanded.

She could only have got hold of a photo of Colin from one of two places: the police or his ex-wife. To be honest, I don't think Colin was bothered that much about it, because he thought, I haven't really done anything wrong.

It *was* my mum behind it all. She had gone round Hull putting up posters saying that Colin was wanted for kidnapping and giving the Crimestoppers phone number. My picture was plastered all over the place as well. She was even going around knocking on strangers' doors saying, 'Do you know this bloke?' She wasn't claming underage sex was going on; she was just wallowing in self-pity, saying, 'He has kidnapped my little girl.' Oh, what a shame she never applied as much effort when Huntley assaulted me.

Colin never kidnapped me. I was the one that kept running back to Hull to be near him, and I was now at Michaela's again, not far from Colin's. Several times she said, 'I'm going to call social services.'

There was one point when I pleaded, 'Please, don't.'

She asked, 'Why?'

I said, 'Because they will just end up picking me up and taking me back.'

I was beginning to understand the consequences of Michaela calling them. To her credit, she told me, 'Hailey, I am getting wise to it now and if this carries on I will put my foot down,' but she still continued to call social services and the police and say, 'Yes, Hailey is here and she is fine.'

By this time, Colin had started a new line of work. He had saved some money from working in the factory, had a phone installed in his house and was now working as a plumber. After a short while, he got a house in a nice area and I moved in with him. We were living together legally now, as I was 16 and Colin had had his bail conditions relaxed so that I could live there.

Before that, Colin had been on bail for supposedly kidnapping me. He was meant to have put me in the back of his car and taped me up. Then the brown stuff hit the fan in a farcical manner, as a direct result of my mum's poster campaign.

Michaela is married to Colin's brother, Ken, and they have a daughter called Louise. There is a similarity between Colin and Ken because they are brothers. There is a third brother Peter, and there is a strong resemblance between all three of the brothers. Anyway, one night before I moved in with Colin, I was upstairs at Michaela's when Louise and her dad got out of the car and skipped into the house.

Vindictively, my mum called the police and said, 'I have just seen Hailey and Colin running into this Michaela's house.'

Next thing, knock, knock, knock, 'Is Hailey here?' It was the police.

'Yes, she is.'

'Where's Colin?' they asked.

Colin's bail conditions at the time were that he should have no contact with me. So what my mum was saying to the police was that he was in breach of these conditions. Although I would like to make it clear that on that particular night I was not with him, and at any other time, whenever there was any contact between us, it was *me* who approached *him*, not the other way around.

What brought all this about was a previous occurrence when I was in Cleethorpes. I'd gone to McDonald's and met up with Colin's brother, Peter, who was with his kids, and he wanted to know how I was getting on.

As it happens, Mum's friend Dawn said she was parked outside McDonald's and that she saw me getting into a car with a man and driving off. She said

I got in the car with Colin. In fact, I had got in the car with Peter.

That was when Colin got arrested. At the time he was staying in a bail hostel in York and it was there, incidentally, that the so-called 'hard men' who branded him the 'paedophile from Hull' attacked him on two separate occasions. Unbeknown to them, the well-spoken, well-groomed man I had come to know had been brought up in the tough back streets of Hull. The son of a hard-living, hard-working and unbreakable fisherman, Colin was well capable of looking after himself. And, for sure, these hard men ended up being wounded far worse in these confrontations than he was.

As a result of being arrested for this further alleged abduction, the next day Colin had to go to York Magistrates' Court to face the charge that he had abducted me for a second time. He was unfairly made to look very bad.

Colin and his solicitor were there in court, but the witnesses were not, and this little old magistrate sitting there with her glasses on asked, 'Where are the witnesses?' She was told, 'They are busy at work.'

The argument put to the court on behalf of Colin was that, if the witnesses were sitting behind the car in question, how could they identify him from the back of his head alone? The magistrate said, 'I am not having a kidnap charge put on him just by identifying somebody by the back of the head. It could have been anybody.

We will leave it on file for the next court case. Go back to your bail hostel.'

The solicitor said that, because Colin had been arrested while staying at the bail hostel, no other bail hostel in the county would take him. This problem was soon solved when his solicitor told the court that Colin's family would take him.

'Whereabouts?' he was asked.

'In Hull, he has got his mum's; he has got his brother's and sister's; he has aunts and uncles.'

The magistrate told the solicitor, 'You pick an address and he can stay there.'

So he did, and all bail restrictions were thrown out. Colin could have his own house again and I was able to live with Colin officially. It was thanks to my mum and Dawn – albeit unwittingly.

Before Colin attended court on the abduction charge, a lot of criticism had been heaped upon him because he appeared in court over a domestic incident with his then wife, Christine. According to Colin, a row between the pair of them flared after she asked Colin to 'chuck' her shoe to her. Instead of passing it, he tossed it across the room so she could catch it, but, he told me, it accidentally caught her on the knee. That is how it all started.

Colin's account was that he said matter-of-factly, 'Oh, sorry, duck. Are you all right?' and that Christine replied, 'Yes, don't worry about it.'

The resultant graze caused to her knee by the shoe was to set in motion a chain of events that would see Colin's unblemished record become tarnished. The week after the shoe-throwing accident, Christine's sister came round to their home and said to Colin, 'You want to keep your hands to yourself, chucking a shoe at my sister.'

In disbelief, Colin said, 'What are you on about?'

'You know, chucking a shoe at my sister,' she said.

Colin innocently admitted, 'Yes, I did. She asked me to chuck her a shoe, so I chucked it.'

She replied, 'Oh! Well, she told me that you got it and you whacked it on her leg.'

Colin ended up going to court because, after he finally split from Christine, he went round to see her one night and took her some shopping. He still took food to her because she had no money.

According to Colin, this time when he called, Christine was in the bath. When she came out she was in her dressing gown and started screaming and shouting. She launched a scathing attack on him, saying, 'What's this I've heard, you're going out with a new girl? What's she like?'

'What can I say?' he replied.

'Well,' Christine pressed him, 'what's she like? What does she look like?'

Colin only fuelled her fire when he began, 'She's a pretty...'

Colin said that Christine cut him short when she

started hurling things across the dining table. Colin, saying he had left his suitcase in the car, went to go out of the front door and, according to Colin, she smacked him in the face three or four times. Colin told me he resisted any temptation to lash out, but, when she punched him in the mouth and bit his thumb, he had no choice but to defend himself and he slapped her across the face.

Subsequently, I saw bite marks on Colin's thumb – it looked like a dog had savaged him. It was the first time he'd hit a woman and he admitted that he shouldn't have done it. 'I was bang out of order for doing it. But she just kept smacking me and smacking me,' he said.

Colin went out to his car but, because he'd had a drink while waiting for her to get out of the bath, he wasn't going to drive the car. He had a clean licence apart from being given penalty points some years earlier for speeding.

As he sat in the car, Colin believed that, even if he did drive off, Christine would phone the police and inform them that he had had a drink. So he took no chances and flung the car keys into some bushes so that he wouldn't be able to drive away.

The only thing he could do was to sit there in the car outside the house. Then there was a tap, tap, tap on the car window. A policewoman was leaning down, looking in, and when Colin wound the window down she told him, 'Colin, you are under arrest for smacking Christine.'

'Why?' he asked.

On smelling alcohol on Colin's breath she added, 'Hang on a minute, you're also under arrest because you are drunk in charge of a vehicle.'

Well, in order to be drunk in charge of a vehicle, you have to have possession of the keys, which of course Colin didn't have.

'I haven't got the keys,' he told her.

Miffed, she said, 'What do you mean, you haven't got the keys?'

He said the car hadn't been locked and he didn't know exactly where the keys were, which was true, of course.

When he finally went to court on these charges, matters were still pending regarding the charges the police lodged against him in respect of abducting me. Here we have a man whose only conviction before all of this was for speeding and now he faced an array of charges that threatened to send his life spiralling out of control.

When Colin appeared in court over the assault against Christine, he stood firm in his plea of not guilty, on the grounds that he did not batter her as she claimed, although he unreservedly admitted slapping her. He admitted this on the basis that they take into consideration what she had done to his face and thumb.

I remember seeing him the day after they had the fight. His mouth was bruised black and blue and his hand still had teeth marks in it.

When we got to court the lawyer said to Colin, 'Have a look at these pictures.'

After viewing them, Colin said to me in a daze, 'Honestly, Hailey, she was black and blue. Her whole face was like... her eye out here, but I never did that. I will put my hand on my heart and I will admit that I did slap her across the face...'

'Right,' I said.

'But only after she had punched me in the mouth four times and bitten my fingers.'

Colin's brother was in court and he said, 'You have got these other charges relating to Hailey pending. What are you going to do?'

Colin said, 'Well, I haven't done that and I am not going to stand there and say I have committed it when I haven't.'

Christine's doctor was called and he confirmed to the court, 'Yes, she came to me.'

Colin wasn't happy about admitting to such an emotive charge. He was adamant that, sometime between him slapping her and the police being called, something else had happened, but he couldn't prove it.

She said that Colin had kicked her in the chest and in the ribs. His lawyer had a point when he said, 'Where are the pictures of her ribs and the pictures of her chest and her back and everything. If she is so black and blue, where are they?'

The reply was: 'She didn't want us to take any pictures.'

'Why not?'

'Well, we don't know.'

So when the judge asked Colin, 'How do you plead?' he reluctantly replied, 'Guilty.' The file in front of the judge was marked 'Not guilty', so this came as a surprise to the judge and he asked Colin, 'Have you changed your plea?'

'Yes I have,' he said.

Then the prosecution stood up and said, 'M'lud, please bear in mind before you say that this man can walk free today that back in 1989 he was driving over the speed limit.'

What that had to do with the seriousness of the charge Colin faced was anyone's guess. But you can bet they didn't wipe that from the records from 1989, though they sure as hell wiped the allegations against Huntley from 1995 onwards.

11
YOU MUST DO THE THING YOU THINK YOU CANNOT DO

THE DISPARITY BETWEEN THE WAY THE POLICE HANDLED THE CHARGE OF UNDERAGE SEXUAL INTERCOURSE, IN RELATION TO ME, AGAINST MY THEN HUSBAND-TO-BE COLIN AND THE WAY THEY HANDLED MY ALLEGATION AGAINST IAN HUNTLEY IS BEYOND COMPREHENSION.

I believe he was able to get the job as a caretaker at a school because he gave his surname as 'Nixon'. He had also put at the bottom of the form 'formerly Huntley', but they did not check that name. This makes me think that having the nerve to put 'formerly Huntley' is a bit like Maxine Carr applying for a credit card and, on being asked, 'Have you ever used a previous name?', answering, 'Maxine Carr.' I don't personally think that you would dare do it if you were carrying that sort of baggage. So when Huntley put that on the form, I think he was lining everything up.

I believe that someone did not put all of the access details from that form into the computer, but, even if they did, it wouldn't show anything anyway. I know the police had apologised for that failure, but that doesn't bring back the dead! Personally, I don't think it was a failure. I think it was a major fuck-up, major because Huntley clearly had blood on his hands.

I was startled when they said they couldn't do anything with forensics or DNA. They said I had left it too long. But they were saying that to a 12-year-old girl. I thought it was my fault; my fault that he couldn't be prosecuted.

I do feel that I have recourse against the police for their failings prior to what Huntley did to me and during their inquiry into my allegation.

Moving on to September 2002, when it was announced that Huntley was to face prosecution for the murders of Holly Wells and Jessica Chapman. We had been keeping a close watch on the TV for news of the police investigation and Colin came in and said, 'Do you mind if I just put the telly on, darling, just to see about these two little girls?' It was odd because just about two weeks before this, for the first time in maybe six months, the name Ian Huntley came into my head. We were passing under a bridge near our home and I couldn't remember if it was Huntley or Hunter, or something like that. Just forget about him, I thought. I don't need that rubbish right now.

I was sitting behind the settee, sorting out a few bits and bobs, and the journalist on the TV announced, 'Today Ian Huntley has been…' and I just stood up and my whole body went into involuntary spasm. I was shaking from head to toe. I couldn't stop.

I could barely get the words out. 'That's him, that's him.'

Colin said, 'What do you mean, "That's him"?'

As if to be sure that it was Huntley, I repeated more clearly, 'That's him.'

'That Ian!' Colin exploded.

'Yes.'

I broke into a screaming fit of blind, incoherent rage. 'That's him. He's obviously done it. Oh my God.' I was going wild. It was as though I couldn't believe what I was seeing. What made it worse was that the news report showed the cunning monster doing TV interviews. I was just so shocked and I ended up ringing my auntie, saying, 'I'm trying to get hold of my mum and her phone is off the hook.' So my uncle went round to my mum's house and said, 'Hailey's trying to get hold of you.'

When I eventually got through to my mum, she started crying and I was just so angry that I burst out, 'I don't know what you're crying for, because nobody gave me the support I needed.'

'Don't say that, we did support you,' she said.

'No, you didn't. You didn't, because you would have had him done, like you tried to have Colin done.'

'Don't say that. Don't say that. That could have been me, you know, just like them parents sat there saying, "My daughter is dead."'

I said, 'Whoop-de-do, that could have been me in the grave. But I am not thinking, Well, that could have been me he did to what he has done to them.'

It was a really stressful time and, to be honest, I don't think words can describe how I felt. That whole day I just couldn't stop shaking. I have never experienced anything like it as an adult. In one way it must have been some sort of spiritual release to know that this now proved that this man was a ticking time bomb waiting to go off, and everybody had the warning signs but I felt they just hadn't listened to me.

I remember, four weeks after meeting Colin, I revealed to him my secret suffering. 'I have been sexually abused,' I said.

Taken aback, he said, 'Crikey! And what got done about that?'

We got into a deeper conversation about it and I said, 'I just wanted to tell people and to have them believe me.'

I just wanted him to give me a hug and say, 'Don't worry,' and that is exactly what Colin did, but that wasn't the reason that I felt love for him.

After we had been together for about a year or so, I

asked him, 'Do you believe me, Colin? Now do you believe me?'

'Of course I believe you. I believed you from the start,' he replied.

He was unfaltering, never doubting me once, whereas a few other people had said, 'Well, are you sure you didn't imagine this?'

'No,' I said to every one of them.

But that is what happened: people thought I had let my imagination run wild. That is one thing Colin never believed. There was not a shadow of a doubt in his mind. Even so, I kept looking for reassurance, or perhaps doubt. 'Do you believe me? Are you sure?'

At this time the press were keen to run a story. Previously, I had refused every time they asked, so as not to lose my pride and dignity. Yet the ever-increasing threats from them that they would print a story with or without my co-operation left me worried that they would print a half-baked version of their own. So I gave them their precious story, but at least it was the truth.

Consequently, when Huntley came to trial, I was asked by the police to give evidence and come forward as a prosecution witness. I received a telephone call, not even a knock at the door, and the conversation was along these lines:

'Hi, is that Hailey?

'Who's calling?'

'My name's Kim and I'm calling from the Cambridgeshire Police.'

'What can I do for you?'

'Obviously, we have heard what happened to you, it is on file. Your complaint in 1997 about what Huntley did to you.'

On hearing the name 'Huntley', I had to hold myself together as the chill of death once again ran down my spine.

I squeezed my insides and managed to cough out, 'Yes.'

'Can I just ask you a few questions?'

'No, I don't want to talk about it, sorry. I'm not interested.'

'Well, why not?'

'Well, are you from the police?'

'Yes.'

'Right, give me your telephone number, give me your special number and wherever you are from and I will call you back just to make sure you are from the police.' It could be anybody, I was thinking.

Obviously, I told Colin and he asked, 'Who was on the phone?'

'It was Kim from the Cambridgeshire Police,' I told him.

He tried to reassure me, saying, 'Keep your head, keep cool. Just relax. Nobody is going to hurt you. Nobody is going to force you into doing anything if you don't want to. If you want to do it, you say yes. If you don't want to do it, say no.'

Kim gave me her telephone number and I got through to the Cambridgeshire Police and asked, 'Could I speak to so-and-so?'

After getting the usual runaround, I asked, 'What's all this about then?'

Back on the phone, Kim defused my anger by starting with: 'Hailey, we just want to ask you a few questions.'

I cautiously asked, 'What about?'

'About the attack that happened on you.'

'Right.'

'I only want to ask you a few questions.'

'And do you expect to get an answer?'

'Why?'

'You want my help?'

'Yes.'

'Well, tough luck because I needed your help four years ago and you did nothing. Nobody was there for me. I was on my own every single night crying my eyes out. I was the one that wet the bed every single night, cut my hair off and started cutting my arms and everything.'

As I spoke, haunting flashbacks ran through my head like ghosts. I was alone, very lost, and now, after all these years, they wanted my help! Two girls murdered, and they even had my details on file. Funny, isn't it, how they had them at hand in readiness for Huntley's trial but not for the vetting of his job application?

No one had cared at that time and here they were

now begging for my help. Their barefaced cheek sent shock waves through my system.

'How dare you call me and ask me this,' I raged.

'Why, is there a problem?' She was pushing her luck.

'OK, let's put it into perspective,' I suggested. 'If your child was to come home, get sexually abused or something like that by the man down the road, I guarantee you would not call in a special unit, you would go and castrate him.'

'I can't comment on that,' was her evasive response.

'You see, and that's because you have got your police badge on. But at the end of the day it's just a nine-to-five job to you.'

If the police liaison unit had been involved, or if it had been a policewoman telling me, 'He deserves everything he gets, pet. We will be behind you and we will get this bastard and we will nail him, even if we have got to do it part-time when we are not getting paid for it,' then I would have stood in the dock for them.

All those years of self-injury, self-abuse, self-denial, self-hatred, self-blame and self-recrimination ruined my childhood, my early teens and my education. Just everything. I have years that can't be replaced. I am not able to retrieve that.

I used self-injury as a coping mechanism to help me overcome the emotional stress that I was incapable of dealing with in any other way. Self-injury was a means of escape, a way to relieve the numbness, and an expression of the pain within me. Something that the police wouldn't care about. They just wanted their day in court, they were desperate to stop the shit hitting the fan, but it was too late… it already had, years earlier.

In no uncertain terms, I told the police to sling their hook, but they weren't having any of it and kept calling me in the hope that I would cave in. They called me on about five occasions in total. This wasn't the 'good cop, bad cop' routine; it was a haunting recurrence of when Huntley persistently abused me.

The police were actually adding to my pain and suffering by pursuing me. If it had been Huntley doing that to me and I had the proof, I would have said, 'Hey, Mr Policeman, Huntley is giving me trouble here,' and then they might have sent him a letter, at the very least.

In one conversation with the police, I said an emphatic no to their request for me to attend Huntley's trial as a prosecution witness. The woman calling me probed sneakily, 'Well, don't you want to help bring this man to justice for doing what he did to Holly and Jessica?'

I snapped, 'There's nothing that would give me more satisfaction than doing that, but, to be honest, there's nothing like rubbing salt in the wound.'

Suddenly, to the police, I had gone from being the centre of an unprovable case to being worth her weight in gold as a star witness in the trial of the decade.

All of a sudden, they were wanting to kiss the hem

of my dress, and I went off on one, telling the woman, 'There is nothing more I would want than to see him stood in the dock and to see him guilty, guilty, guilty. Right you are, off to prison for however many years.

'I will come to court the day you prosecute him for what he did to me. Let me stand up there and prove what he did to me and be believed and then I will help you. You help me and I will help in return.'

At this, she soon changed her tune, blurting out, 'We can't, because the case file has been misplaced,' and giving me all these rubbish excuses.

I finished curtly, 'In which case, the answer is no. I needed your help many years ago and I didn't get anything.'

By this time, Colin was facing abduction charges – the unlawful sexual intercourse charge had not yet been put to him – relating to when we had gone off for a couple of weeks. The fact that the police were causing more unnecessary turmoil in my life by prosecuting the man I love caused me a lot of additional anger. I would lick mud off his boots and, to be honest, he would do the same for me because we are as close as that and nobody can come between us. People keep trying to but it just makes our resolve to ride it out stronger.

There is a major thing that happened in Colin's life when he was younger that he can't understand, but he can see where I am coming from because what happened to me was like what happened to him and, be assured, the man I love will take that to his grave.

How I take things now is that I try to look to the future, but I am best dealing with things day by day. How I suffered at the hands of a family friend. How I coped with the immense pain of feeling dramatically let down and for Colin to have been pursued over a matter I had not complained of, when Huntley escaped similar charges, albeit he had not been pursued by a complainant, I do not know.

The impact on my life and other people's lives is immeasurable. How do you make the police change? How do you make them pay? How on earth could they make it right for me? I'll tell you how: by getting off their backsides. The police at ground level do a grand job, but the decision makers need to be taken to task for what happened in my case. If I sound bitter, that's because I *am* bitter.

Although they have punished and sent Huntley to prison for what he did to Holly and Jessica, are all the other victims just supposed to go, 'Oh well, he's not going to do that any more, he's in prison for the rest of his life'? Because of that, are we supposed to just forget about it and not worry about it?

I will have my day with Huntley, mark my words. I want him to be as scared and as frightened and worried thinking about what's going to happen to him as I was that day that he was doing that to me.

I want to see the whites of his eyeballs when I bring that action against him, for I must do what the police and the CPS failed to do. In the words of Eleanor Roosevelt: 'You must do the thing you think you cannot do.'

How scared do I think Huntley will be to be taken from the safety of his prison? As fucking scared as I was when he said he would kill me. I think in his psychotic little mind that he believes that one day he is going to get out of prison. I too honestly believe that one day he will walk away from that prison. And it is now my mission to stop him. I believe that is possible.

I still have nightmares. In fact, I had one that was the most real-to-life feeling. Huntley had been released because he had been given a drug that had rehabilitated him. He was back, working in society, and he had built himself up. He was given this drug, let out for the weekend and had to be brought back on the Monday morning, and this was the Saturday night. Somehow, the scheming molester had found out my address and he came to my house.

Unaware of his weekend out of prison, I was at home alone. I think it was scarier because Colin wasn't there. I was upstairs. I pushed the bedroom door shut, pulled the curtains across the window and I was just lying in bed watching the telly when, all of sudden, I heard the floor downstairs creak. I jumped up and my whole body started shaking uncontrollably, the same shake as that day I found out that Huntley had been arrested over Holly and Jessica. I opened the door and I stood there thinking, Is it just me being paranoid? Don't worry about it, it *is* just me being paranoid, I'm always doing this.

I heard another creak and I jumped out of my skin. It was him and he came up the stairs. The crazed, ghoulish look was back in his eyes and I had nothing but abject fear in mine. I managed to gasp, 'What are you doing here?' He said, 'I'm here to be your friend now.' He was coming out with all this Jekyll and Hyde rubbish. 'I'm sorry for what I did, mate. I'll be your mate now, your best friend. I've been taking these special drugs and, you know, I'm going to get a job now. I'm really sorry.'

Suddenly, I just pushed him and blasted at him, 'Get away from me,' and then he turned on me, dragged me into the bedroom and did what he had done to me in real life, and then he got up.

To some degree, and I know this sounds strange, I think the evil essence of Huntley still pervades places where I am. Call it autosuggestion, call it what you want, but that is how evil Huntley is.

When he enticed Holly and Jessica into his caretaker's house, I reckon they scratched and kicked and screamed to get away, whereas I cowered in the corner begging for my life. In my opinion, Huntley sexually abused those girls. With Huntley, it was all about control; the sexual acts were secondary to that. This, I believe, was the only way he could become aroused. I think he has some sort of physical or psychological problem where he could only physically abuse, sexually abuse, before he could get any gratification. This is what I felt when he was abusing me, that he was not becoming aroused and he was not genuinely gaining anything for himself other than getting the power, through sexual abuse, that in turn aroused him. It was sexual power.

In the two agonising hours in that secluded orchard, he tried to brainwash me in order to get that control, to have that power over me.

I felt that tightening grip of his evil persistence, wearing and grinding me down. This, I think, is what he could have done with Holly and Jessica. That he would have tried to grind them down. He could have said to one of them, 'If you leave, I'll strangle her right now.' I think he did that to those girls.

I believe that the fact that Huntley escaped the consequences of his vile attack on me allowed him to penetrate deep into the heart of his obsessions without fear of being caught. He convinced himself that there was no way he could be caught and he went ahead and disposed of his victims' bodies. He must have been laughing at the police. Well, let's see who has the last laugh now.

12

A SNAKE IN THE GRASS

COLIN'S TRIAL FOR SUPPOSEDLY ABDUCTING ME WAS
LISTED AS A FOUR-WEEK HEARING, BUT IT WAS CUT
SHORT DRAMATICALLY ON THE DAY OF THE HEARING.
We went to court in the morning and all of my family
were there. And there were all these people there who
were willing to give statements as to how they saw
Colin bundle me into the back of his car and all sorts
of silly things.

In the pre-hearing meeting the night before the
trial, Colin's lawyer, Lloyd Edwards, explained that he
had seen DC Condon and DC Fell in the police
station one night recently.

Colin, none the wiser, said, 'Oh, right.'

These were the people who made the comments to

Colin when he first handed himself in that night, like, 'I knew I would get hold of you' and 'I knew I would find you', so obviously they had taken a dislike to him.

The lawyer went on, 'They said they are going to have you for underage sex when you leave court.'

'Yes,' said Colin.

After catching his breath, the lawyer continued, 'They're going to rearrest you for underage sex and have you done for it and then, in the morning, when you go to court, they are going to put it to the court as well.'

It was explained to Colin that the Prosecution were offering a deal. 'If you admit you had underage sex with Hailey, you walk free from the court today and you will not get arrested tonight when you leave this very courtroom or anything like that. You will probably get a fine and you will be put on the Sex Offenders' Register.'

Defence counsel John Thackray told the court that Colin had not known how old I was at the time of the disappearance. He also made it clear that no complaint had ever been made by me against Colin and that we continued to live together in a stable relationship. 'They are doing well in life,' he said to the court. 'He is in full-time work and supports her.'

In February 2003, Colin walked from court and escaped a prison sentence. Instead, he was placed on the Sex Offenders' Register for five years after admitting having unlawful sex with me between 1 December 2001 and February 2002. He was also handed a three-year conditional discharge and £960 costs. Oh, and as for the abduction charges, Judge Trevor Barber ordered two further counts of abducting a child to lie on file.

When we came out of court, we went into the Duke of Wellington, behind the court, to have a celebratory drink. In the pub, we saw my mum, my dad and a few others walk in, and we started having a few drinks. Then, inexplicably, my dad got hold of Colin and said, 'Welcome, mate. You made the right choice in doing what you are doing.'

The very same people who had been prepared to give evidence against Colin were now having to save face. To Colin and me, they said, 'Of course, we didn't want you to go to prison, that is not what we wanted.'

My mum was insincere when she bragged, 'I was sitting with the judge.' Oh, yeah, 'Hi, mister judge, can I come and sit with you? My name is Mandy Edwards.'

Somehow I don't think so. I do know the lawyers went to sit with the judge and the prosecution went as well, but that was when they sorted out the deal.

Just as some members of my family had betrayed me, so did a close friend who had come to stay with Colin and me for a while around this time. I took this person – whose identity I cannot reveal for legal reasons – out on a shopping spree. My bank card was always on the sideboard, but I had another bank card that I didn't use, just in case I lost the first one.

With this friend living with us now, I felt uncomfortable about telling him to look away when I got money out of the cash machine, but when he was by my side I guess he cottoned on to my pin number. And then one day he took Colin's car from outside the house, leaving a note that said, 'I have borrowed your car, I hope you don't mind.' The cheek of it! He hadn't even passed his driving test. 'I will bring it back on Monday,' he had added. This was on the Saturday.

Colin was on tenterhooks. 'Oh, for God's sake, I don't need this,' he said. If this bloke was out drink-driving and ran somebody down, obviously ownership of the car would be traced back to Colin.

By chance, my dad had seen this friend at the petrol station in Colin's car and said, 'What are you doing in that car?'

'Colin let me use it,' he said.

'I don't think so,' Dad said, and drove the car back to my so-called friend's house and called Colin to say, 'Don't you let this young lad drive your car.'

Colin was flabbergasted and told him, 'I never. He took it and I've got the note here to prove that he said, "I have borrowed your car, I hope you don't mind and I will bring it back on Monday."'

Dad said, 'Right, you come and pick up this car from his parents' house.'

The snake had returned to his parents' house without a word and two days later Colin picked up the car. I had arranged to go shopping in Meadowhall, in Sheffield, and when we got there I went to the cash machine to draw out some money. I entered my pin and twice the message came up, 'Incorrect pin number'. I thought, How can that be an incorrect pin number, I've had it for ages? On my third attempt the machine sucked my card in.

I sensed something was amiss. I had pampered this bloke with thousands of pounds' worth of stuff. I wasn't rich, but I had just come into a few thousand pounds compensation money and wanted to put a little cheer back into his life. Little did I know that he would be a snake in the grass. Obviously, he had got hold of my spare card.

I called him after the weekend and asked, 'Have you got this card?'

His reply didn't surprise me. 'Yes.'

I said, 'Right, OK. I need to come and get the card as I need some money out of the bank.'

'OK,' he said, and Colin and I met up with him.

Knowing something underhand had gone on, I walked into the bank and asked, 'Can I have a statement of what money has been taken out of my account, please?'

As I read through the statement, I saw £30 had been spent on petrol for the car, £10 on a pair of cheap shoes, and then my eyes opened in stark disbelief as I realised £500 cash had been withdrawn, and, with this and other expenditure I couldn't account for, the total amount withdrawn was about £1,500, if not a few hundred pounds more.

I got back in the car where he was sitting. He was shaking like a leaf and I looked at Colin and he knew straight away what I was going to say. 'Can I ask you something?'

'Yes,' he replied sheepishly.

'Just be honest with me,' I told him. 'Have you taken any money out of my account with my card?'

The conniving snake sat there shaking, with a dreamy look about him as he blurted out, 'Oh, yes. I... I... borrowed five hundred quid in June, so I could go on holiday with my girlfriend.'

I was incandescent with rage as I said, 'Well, it would have been nice if you had asked me before you took my card and withdrew that money.' Then I thought, I'll have to keep him sweet, otherwise he won't pay me my money back.

Making a mockery of my previous generosity, he made a paltry offer, 'I'll pay you five pounds a week out of my Giro, OK?'

I held back my anger as I said, 'That's fine.' Well, it's better that than nothing, I thought.

We went back to his parents' house because he said he had a little bit of money there. I thought, That must be the other £1,000 that is missing out of my account, that he has got upstairs. As it turned out, he had been out on an all-weekend bender with his friends. I was mega-annoyed, thinking, You've been spending my money from all the crap that I went through and that money was for my benefit in a way. I took him in and he ripped me off.

I did report the matter to the police but once again was told that there wasn't enough evidence to pursue the matter further. I shrugged it off and thought, Fine, every dog has his day. What comes around goes around. To this day, he has not repaid a penny of the money he stole from me. It may as well have gone down the drain. Gone in a weekend, £1,500 in a weekend. I could understand it if he had something to show for it, but he didn't, he just spent it all on drink. He denied it and said that I had given him permission to use my account – my word against his.

By this time, my relationship with my mum and dad was so-so. To some small degree, they accepted Colin, but behind closed doors they were saying, 'We don't like Colin.' They were putting on a show.

I believe my dad had said that he liked him because they used to go to the bookies' together. Colin would just put a couple of quid in the fruit machine because he thinks it is a waste of money, whereas my dad would put £500 in and Colin would be amused by that. 'Five hundred quid! You must be mad. Five hundred quid in a machine and it pays out something like four hundred. You are nuts, you are losing. No, no, no.' My dad was a fruit-machine addict, the gambler that would be left with nothing.

The only bit of good news to come out of it was when, out of the blue, in October 2003, Colin received a letter from the Humberside Police about his name being on the Sex Offenders' Register. Amazingly, common sense prevailed in a letter from PC Longstaff and PC Smales that said, 'We have been discussing your case for some time in relation to the court placing you on the Sex Offenders' Register when you were convicted in February this year. After consulting with our legal department and other forces, we have been advised that because you received a conditional discharge you should not have to register.'

Colin had had to go and sign on this register and tell them where he lived and all the rest of it. This was all done in front of the court and the papers had written about it, but the police weren't prepared to go to the press and say, 'Fine, we are taking him off this register because we feel he is not a danger.'

To Colin, that letter more than made his day. But then he had had no reason to be labelled with that tag in the first place. Yet Huntley can be the subject of numerous allegations and even then alarm bells didn't ring.

Colin had been branded a 'sex offender' but he shouldn't have even been on the Sex Offenders' Register. The police had made another blunder and because of it Colin's name was sullied in all the newspapers and on the internet. At least it has been disclosed here that they gave him an apology.

13

ABUSE VICTIMS' TIME
BEHIND SCARS

JUST ABOUT EVERY GIRL DREAMS OF HAVING A CHURCH WEDDING. All our trouble behind us – well, sort of – we married on the afternoon of 3 July 2004 at St Peter's Church, in Humberston, with the Reverend Brian East officiating.

What marred our wedding to some degree were the veiled allegations and threats from certain members of my family before the day, but, all in all, I was relieved to end up in the arms of the man who really cares for me. At long last, we'll spend our lives together, I told myself.

Of course, we were head over heels in love with each other and had never been so happy. And I don't think I would be alive today if it wasn't for Colin's normality. There are only a few people that are normal, I've decided.

Although Mum and Dad attended the wedding, none of my brothers was invited and, thankfully, none came to offer their blessing. Because of the press interest, we decided not to have a massive gathering. A lot of things were said, but, that aside, it was the best day of my life. There were many emotions running through me as we said our vows and, not surprisingly, I was very nervous, knowing that the world's press were waiting outside to get a snap of us. Well, just like *Hello!* fiercely protects its wedding photos, Colin and I somehow managed to sneak to our limousine without any of them actually getting a photo of us. I had now become Mrs Giblin. It was what I had longed for, and the fairytale wedding I had dreamed of was now complete.

This was the first time that I felt loved and cherished. Colin used to say, 'Nobody will ever touch a hair on your head, because I would be the one hurting them.' I felt the safest I had been and the most secure. Obviously, it has everything to do with our love and the happiness, but we have developed such a strong bond of unity that nobody could break it, although some evil people keep trying.

Those trying to break the bond are family and ex-friends and people who judge us. While they are wasting their time judging our relationship, it's really their relationships that are falling to pieces, not ours.

We're not just soul mates and lovers, we're best friends, and we don't let anybody come between us.

I know that some people might consider the age difference between Colin and me to be a problem, but I don't think that age has got anything to do with it. Some people may disagree, but you can't help who you fall in love with. I could be with somebody who is my age, go through all the trouble and all the things coming out in the press about Huntley and my husband's finding out about it, and he might not be strong-minded enough to cope.

I don't want to be involved with some young thug more interested in swilling booze, hitting the drugs or out there just nicking cars and breaking into old people's houses and causing trouble on a Saturday night.

I would prefer to sit at home with a bottle of wine, chatting on a Saturday night. That is the way I enjoy myself. I like living the fast life but, sometimes, when it gets too fast, I need to slow down a bit and think about what I am doing.

Having added stability to my life, I decided to take steps to bring closure to a part of my life that would otherwise always haunt me. In August 2004, having written a letter to the Humberside Police telling them how unhappy I was at the treatment I had received and how they conducted the inquiry in 1998, I received a letter from Detective Chief Superintendent Gavin Baggs. This outlined the form of the inquiry into

Huntley that the police would undertake at my request.

I feel they have breached my human rights by putting me through this for a year and it has left me feeling very bitter. It was probably the worst day of my life. I felt like a disbelieved 11-year-old all over again!

The police promised to return paperwork, which has not been returned to me at the time of writing, late 2005. However, what they did give to me was far more sacred than paperwork: the police interview of me from 1998, on videotape. Some readers may have seen extracts of the video interview on *ITN News* on British ITV and many European news channels. What I said in that lip-biting, stomach-churning interview as a child was pretty damaging.

I now feel that the only line of attack that I have left to bring closure to this ordeal is to have Huntley sentenced in court for what he did to me. Even if it were only a light token sentence, it would make me happy to think, Yes, now you are getting punished because you are spending that extra day in prison because of me. It's because of what you did to me that you are being punished.

At present, I feel that he's just laughing in the face of the police. No doubt this book will provoke some comment from them, even if in private, and I want that comment to be aimed at Huntley, not me. Remember, it is Huntley who caused all this, not me.

Right now he's in his cell and he's laughing; he knows

he's a celebrity convict, a trophy to be held aloft for all to see, while in private he will get all he demands, even bottles of vodka. And, if in 25 years' time they come up with some wonder drug that can curb what these evil monsters do, then he could be out even sooner than 40 years from now – just as in my nightmare.

On the other hand, if I were to kill him, would I get 25 years in prison and would I be branded the same? If I were to see him in the street, I wouldn't be able to control myself. I don't want this man to be freed in 40 years' time, but neither do I want him dead. I want his living hell to continue for as long as my living hell goes on. I want him to be kept alive for as long as I am living my nightmare.

However, I do fear that there is a likelihood that he could eventually be freed. In order to stop that from happening, I would like to hammer home the final nail in his coffin by bringing a private criminal prosecution, which I am allowed to do. But only time will tell if I do.

Huntley hates the word 'paedophile' and says, 'I'm no paedophile.' Well, plainly, he *is* a paedophile. By putting your hands into a little girl's knickers in a sexual way, that is what you are, and, if you don't want to be classed as that, don't do it.

This man considers himself to be a different type of criminal. He thinks that he is a celebrity, and he is relying on that celebrity status to make things happen. He knows if he threatens to kill himself they will jump for him, as they don't want him dead. He knows if he so much as coughs the press will be there to pick it up. It's his way of exerting control, and he's still at it.

I often wonder, What if they reintroduced capital punishment? No, hanging's too easy and it's too quick. I want people to walk past him and take chunks off him, or somebody to do something to him that would give him nightmares, but to make him pay and to hurt him mentally, physically, every way that you possibly could, the way that he did to me. Most of my scars are on the inside. I'm still a living victim. I haven't recovered. I don't think I will.

The girls that came forward at the time have made complaints, but our screams for help fell on deaf ears, on cold hearts; that's how I see it.

Right now I just want a normal, peaceful life with no screaming and shouting, nobody there unless I feel safe with them and nobody to ever hurt me again. I want to stand up and fight and be the independent person that I am.

Most abuse victims have the feeling of self-blame: I've been sexually abused and nobody will want me now. I would like to help them by example to show that the feeling of self-worth can be restored. To those who have suffered sexual abuse of any sort, I say there is always light at the end of the tunnel.

I have great respect for those working with children that are going off the rails. I would like to tell them my story or for them to read my book and I hope that it will go on to inspire them to know that life doesn't stop just because of the abuse they have suffered. I know this has happened to me. I have had years and years of torment and troubles, but one day I will be able to grow up strong and further my career in whatever I want to do. You can be somebody rather than just sit and think that your life has come to an end. Have faith.

For all the victims out there, have a voice and if the police try to fob you off with 'Sorry, we don't have enough evidence', just keep fighting. You have a right to fight. While paedophiles, abusers and their kind are out there, we all have to fight them. Even women who have put up with it for 30 years, try to put your foot down and think, I don't want this to happen to my siblings, my children and my friends' children or to anybody else. To have a voice and keep shouting and shouting and shouting until somebody listens is what is important, and that is what I intend to do.

I also want to embark on a lingerie-modelling career to show the world that, just because you have been a victim, you don't necessarily have to be pushed around by someone who ruined your childhood. I still want a career in modelling, not to prove to anybody else, but to prove to myself, that I am capable of doing something that I enjoy doing and, hopefully, be an inspiration to other children, to other sufferers, other victims. I will always stand proud for who and what I am.

Something came to my notice during the course of my creating this book; it was a newspaper headline that read: 'Disgraced officer to face "hell of all hells"'. This was to do with the disgraced Soham Inquiry police officer Detective Constable Brian Stevens, who gave the police a false alibi when faced with allegations that he downloaded child porn to his laptop.

I read with concern that the family of Jessica Chapman said that they felt betrayed that Stevens, their liaison officer, used their grief to bolster up his defence in his trial at the Old Bailey, which may have helped him secure the rather lenient prison sentence of eight months for conspiring to pervert the course of justice.

What made matters worse for me was when I read of the involvement of a female executive officer for the CPS, Louise Austin, who provided the alibi for Stevens. She was given a six-month prison sentence, suspended for two years.

This 'hell of all hells' Stevens was meant to be facing pales into insignificance compared with the pain endured by an abuse victim. At least Stevens was released from his prison sentence. Abuse victims never escape their time behind scars.

Grandly betraying the trust placed in him by family members when he was asked to read a poem at the celebration of life service at Ely Cathedral, he tainted for ever what should have been a poignant reminder of Jessica Chapman's life.

So many lives have been ruined by the acts of Huntley, a wantonly evil man, and all those he came into contact with bear some type of psychological scarring. I have made little mention of Maxine Carr, who lied for Huntley and now she pays the price, for ever a prisoner to those circumstances, always in need of constant protection from the threat of violence that shadows her closely guarded life.

In drawing your attention to my story, I hope I have shown the sensationalism attached to Huntley and how he has achieved the ultimate power that he never gained before.

Huntley will not be considered for release from prison until he is 69. This was decreed by High Court judge Mr Justice Moses, who ordered that he must serve a minimum sentence of at least 40 years – minus the 14 months he spent on remand before his trial.

This long-awaited announcement had been delayed because Huntley's trial ended when the law relating to the setting of prison tariffs was changing.

Mr Justice Moses said, 'His actions in pretending to exhibit innocent concern after the murders demonstrate his lack of remorse.'

Although the judge emphasised, 'I have not ordered that this defendant will not spend the rest of his life in prison,' this did not mean that he would not spend the rest of his life in prison.

I am younger, stronger and a born fighter, and one

day I will see the whites of Ian Huntley's eyes, and, although he has locked me behind bars, incarcerated me, for the rest of my life, we have that in common, but I have the key to my cell door, which he can never again close on me.

I want to 'rid' myself of the tag 'Huntley's Victim'. I know that real people like and respect me for being me – Hailey Giblin. Ian Kevin Huntley was born a bastard and will die a bastard. I used to think that I needed him to admit his crimes for me to obtain the closure I desperately longed for.

When I had almost finished writing this book, something dawned on me, and I now understand that this was just another hold Huntley had over me and his other victims. So I have a message for you, Ian Huntley: one day, I will see the whites of your eyes once more and we can then do it the easy way or the hard way. And, finally, I don't need your admission of guilt to feel believed. Your selfish, perverted actions spoke louder than words.

Now, too, I realise that some of the contents of this book may well hurt some people. I can only be me and I can only be honest, and, for being just that, I am sorry.

At the end of 2005, I asked the Humberside Police Force for witness statements and case notes relating to my attack from 1998, plus the statements that were also taken in 2005, so that I could pursue a private prosecution against Huntley. They told me that they had to write to each witness to gain their consent for the witness statements could be released to me.

I was sent a copy of their letter to the witnesses, which read:

RE: HAILEY JAYNE GIBLIN
(FORMERLY EDWARDS)

You will recall that you previously gave a statement to Humberside Police in connection with the investigation of allegations made by Hailey Giblin that in 1997 she was a subject of a sexual assault by Ian Huntley. As you will no doubt know, Ian Huntley was more recently convicted of the murders of Holly Wells and Jessica Chapman in Soham in 2002.

The allegations made by Mrs Giblin in relation to Ian Huntley have been the subject of further police investigation and the papers have been re-submitted to the Crown Prosecution Service. The CPS, having considered the evidence, has declined to prosecute.

Mrs Giblin has indicated that she wishes to issue a private prosecution against Ian Huntley and has asked Humberside Police to supply her with the papers generated in the course of its investigation. These papers of course include the statement taken from you.

The purpose of this letter is therefore to ask you whether you give your consent to the disclosure of your statement to Mrs Giblin for the purposes of her proposed private prosecution of Ian Huntley.

I am enclosing a form of response which I would be grateful if you could complete, sign and date, and return to me in the sae provided.

I am anxious to respond to Mrs Giblin as soon as possible and your early reply would be very much appreciated.

I should say that were a private prosecution to proceed, and were you to be called as a witness, the procedure, and more particularly your own involvement in the process, would be very much the same as if the prosecution were being brought by the CPS.

I hope the position is clear and I look forward to hearing from you.

Yours sincerely

Stephen Hodgson
Head of Legal Services

You may notice that the author of this letter writes that the papers concerning my case were re-submitted to the CPS but the information before the Bichard Inquiry was that the papers were not submitted to the CPS.

Subsequently, a letter from Detective Chief Superintendent Gavin Baggs was sent to Stephen Richards (my co-author), in response to him asking for information about my case. Dated 14th June 2005, here is a telling extract from it:

'Whilst I am not in a position to answer specific questions about the investigation you will be aware that the Humberside Police made a submission about this case to the Bichard Inquiry. That submission should be available to you via the Bichard website.

I can confirm that the case was passed to the Crown Prosecution Service at the conclusion of police investigation in 1998 and that the decision not to proceed with the prosecution was made by the CPS.'

Bullshit is what I say to that – the information before the Bichard Inquiry was that the case file never actually reached the CPS as it was the police who decided not to prosecute Huntley. It was DCI Baggs who, before a meeting in 2004, asked me to sign a confidentiality agreement, to prevent me from disclosing any of the contents of the meeting to any third parties. My lawyers advised me not to sign any such document.

Three weeks later, Stephen Hodgson, the lawyer from the Humberside Police, contacted me to say that he had had a telephone conversation with a witness in the case, Jackie Blakey (Katie Webber's mother) who said that she would not release her statement to me. I could not help but ask myself why.

A few days later, my loving brother Hayden indicated on his release form 'under no circumstances whatsover' for his statement to be released – again, why?

As far as I know, Katie Webber has decided not to contact the lawyer at the police and has not responded in any way. James Webber, Katie's brother has also decided to ignore the request.

This is why our justice system fails and this is also *another* reason why child killers and paedophiles can slip through the net.

Obviously, I was upset and angry as to why these witnesses wouldn't allow their statements to be used in court to prosecute the bastard.

Subsequently, I tried to contact Jackie and Katie. They were not able to come to the phone, so I spoke to Katie's Nana, Shirley Blakey.

After saying 'Hello', Shirley immediately made it crystal clear that none of the family would release their statement. I was brutally attacked by a future child killer and that had ruined my childhood – what about justice?

In due course, the force solicitor confirmed the following to me:

'I confirm that I have had no response whatsoever to my most recent letters to Katie Webber or James Webber. I think I must now conclude that they do not wish to co-operate. I believe that one or more of my letters must have come to their attention. Failure to respond at all suggests to me that they simply do not wish to engage with the process. Without any response from them explaining their position, I can do little more to pursue this matter ...'

Obviously, I made my feelings clear. I said that when my book is released the truth would finally be told.

Stephen Hodgson, Head of Legal Services at the Humberside Police *again* contacted both me and the publishers of this book, pressing for sight of the copy. He wanted to know that the 'contents are fair and accurate and do not defame any individuals within Humberside Police'.

In my opinion, The Bichard Report was most fair and accurate. Were the police as diligent as they should have been when I encountered Huntley? Did Huntley live a charmed existence or is there another explanation? Time will tell. But then again, that's another story ...

EPILOGUE

It has taken some time for me to write this book and it has helped me most certainly to come to terms with how lucky I am to be alive. I now have my beautiful family to grow old with and a future that seems to get better day by day. A future that I could only once dream of is now becoming a reality and sharing this story with the world has lifted a huge weight off my shoulders – now people can make their own judgement about me once and for all.

I now plan to travel, to move on from a sad past to a bright future and to make myself successful because I think I deserve it. I think now it's time to spoil myself and leave behind an inevitable spotlight that fell upon me that was, frankly, never asked for.

My final aim in life is to see that my children never have to grow up as quickly as I did. And I leave you with my final thought: Yesterday has been, and yesterday has gone, I live for today because I have won.

CHILDLINE

IF YOU ARE A CHILD OR YOUNG PERSON NEEDING HELP PLEASE CALL OUR FREE 24-HOUR HELPLINE ON 0800 1111. Lines can be busy but please keep trying and you will get through.

If you are deaf or find using a regular phone difficult, try our Textphone service which provides confidential support and advice via a Textphone. You can call on 0800 400 222 and it's open from 9.30am to 9.30pm on weekdays and 9.30am to 8pm at weekends.

We also provide a special helpline called The Line for any young person living away from home. This is the helpline for you if you live in a foster home or a children's home, if you're at boarding school or you've been in hospital for a long time. You can call The Line on 0800 884444 from 3.30pm to 9.30pm on weekdays and 2pm to 8pm at weekends.

To make a donation, go to www.childline.org.uk